AF441833

Trading The US Markets

A Comprehensive Guide to US Markets for International Traders and Investors

by Paolo Pezzutti

HARRIMAN HOUSE LTD

3A Penns Road
Petersfield
Hampshire
GU32 2EW
GREAT BRITAIN

Tel: +44 (0)1730 233870
Fax: +44 (0)1730 233880
Email: enquiries@harriman-house.com
Website: www.harriman-house.com

First published in Great Britain in 2008
Copyright © Harriman House Ltd

ISBN 978-1-905641-05-5

British Library Cataloguing in Publication Data
A CIP catalogue record for this book can be obtained from the British Library.

Printed and bound by Athenaeum Press Limited, Tyne & Wear

To my lovely daughters Carla and Livia, and my wife Caterina.
Thanks to Carlo, who made me understand the concept of risk.

Contents

Preface

What the book covers

Trading the U.S. Markets provides a guide for European traders and investors to the complex and fascinating universe of the U.S. exchanges. In order to provide the reader with the knowledge necessary to approach the biggest capital market in the world, this book describes the market's characteristics, the mechanics of choosing a broker and opening an account in the U.S.

It is not easy to make these choices without knowing the many possibilities you have. As trading implies risk, traders and investors have to be aware of these risks and make their judgments based on sound and transparent information. Having access to the best sources of information can provide great support. Being a good trader also requires knowing in detail the mechanics of a trade and the market structure, plus the rules and procedures adopted by the exchanges. Risks and opportunities associated with the different market dynamics and structures can make the difference. In this book you will find information about the impact of the bid/ask spread on your strategies and the explanation of concepts like volatility, liquidity and stop loss. Market behavior changes over time and even the different trading hours have specific characteristics. Part-time traders can benefit from opportunities offered by technology to compete with professionals in terms of analysis capabilities and speed of execution.

Who the book is for

This book is written for individual traders and investors who want to approach the U.S. markets. Everyone from beginners to more advanced traders can find useful information about the different market structures and dynamics. The variety of products and alternatives available offers great possibilities, but, at the same time, can be quite disorienting if approached without the necessary knowledge and tools. Nowadays, technology allows European traders to access U.S. markets without any delay or disadvantage with respect to traders located in the U.S. Trading from Europe, with the benefit of low commissions and the low cost of technology, holds a great deal of potential.

The information provided in this book can be useful for those who want to explore the different exchange characteristics, the financial instruments to be traded, the availability of software platforms and sources of information. The time-zone difference between Europe and the U.S. is a great opportunity for European part-time traders who can trade markets in the afternoon and in the evening after work.

How the book is structured

This book is divided into three parts. The first part provides an overview of the U.S. markets. It describes the main U.S. exchanges, regional exchanges, the Electronic Communication Networks (ECNs), and the bulletin boards, together with the main characteristics of order- and quote-driven markets, and floor and electronic trading. The main financial products available for you to invest or trade are described together with the market's characteristics in terms of flow of information, transparency, market hours, settlement rules, liquidity and volatility.

The second part of the book looks at the mechanics you need to know to be able to trade U.S. markets. Here, you will find some useful information about the different types of brokers and software platforms available. I will describe the requirements to open an account in the U.S. and how to fund and access your account online. A description of the main risks associated with trading because of losses and fraud is also important to make sound decisions. Finally, I describe the sources of information about trading and investing you can find on the web, in magazines, and on blogs and forums.

The third and last part looks at the mechanics of a trade. Starting with how to enter your trading account, the book will guide you through your first trade in practice, describing concepts such as bid/ask, the various types of orders, and the characteristics of the trading day through open, mid-session and close. You will also find some information on how to take advantage of the time difference between the U.S. and Europe, and the risk and opportunities of program and automated trading.

Introduction: Why Trade the U.S. Markets

Trading U.S. markets represents an excellent opportunity for European traders. Nowadays, it is possible to trade U.S. stocks on European exchanges and you can trade U.S. markets by opening an account with a European broker. These are viable and legitimate choices for traders. However, you can also consider opening an account with a U.S. broker to directly trade U.S. markets, enjoying the benefits of low commissions and fees and an environment of transparent and fair competition between exchanges. Low commissions are an excellent reason to do it. Generally, it is more expensive to buy a U.S. stock using a European platform than doing it through a U.S. broker.

Market diversification, with the largest number of financial products and listed companies in the world, is another reason to look with interest at U.S. markets. Regulation is very well regarded in the U.S. Although the U.S. markets have been badly hit by the well-known post-dot.com bubble scandals, regulators have acted promptly and efficiently to protect investors. Accessing U.S. markets is simple. You can open your account and transfer your funds very easily. Of course, you have to comply with legal and tax requirements, but once you have made these simple steps, you are ready to access markets online, the same way you access your domestic market. The range of tradable instruments and the greatest access to financial information available on the web allows traders to experience a favorable trading environment. On average, customer support provided by brokers presents a high standard. The time difference is also quite important to part-time European traders. At the time they return home from work, U.S. markets are usually choppy during the lunch hours. Thus, European traders can enjoy the last "power" hour right after their European dinner.

Given the explanations provided, the aim of this book is to encourage you to consider U.S. markets for your trading. At the very least, I hope that the information I have provided will help you make sound judgments about your trading decisions – where to trade, what to trade, when to trade and how to trade – being aware of the risks and opportunities associated to trading.

PART I:

Basics – Overview of the U.S. Markets

Exchanges

Background of U.S. markets (NYSE, NASDAQ, AMEX, CBOE, CBOT, CME, NYMEX, NYBOT KCBT, OneChicago, MGEX, ISE exchanges)

Stock exchanges provide a market for buying and selling shares of companies. They are regulated by the Securities and Exchange Commission (SEC) and play an extremely important role in the U.S. economy. Each exchange provides the regulatory oversight and the facilities in which the brokers work, and acts as a self-regulatory organization complying with the rules established by the SEC to provide a fair trading environment. Most of the exchanges' members are broker-dealer organizations. Rules and trading technologies differ significantly from one exchange to another and evolve at a fast pace, while exchanges have initiated an impressive process of reorganization.

The National Market System was established by Congress in 1975 to promote competition among exchanges and allow investors to get the best possible price regardless of where the order is executed.

Competition has accelerated a consolidation trend, which is still ongoing not only at the U.S. level, but globally with U.S. exchanges trying to expand their influence in Asia and Europe. The trend of mergers and partnerships is occurring in a competitive environment characterized by low margins and expensive technology innovations. The U.S. exchanges' structure is challenged by fierce competition not only within the nation, but also from Asian and European exchanges.

As an example of this trend, when you look at the distribution of IPO activity among regions and stock exchanges in 2006, Europe's exchanges raised 39% of the total capital (US$95 billion). Thanks to Chinese listings, Asia-Pacific raised 35% (US$85.5 billion). North America's exchanges were only third with 19% (US$46.3 billion). Analyzing individual stock exchanges, the Hong Kong Stock Exchange (HKSE) raised 19% of global capital (US$46.1 billion), the London Stock Exchange (LSE) was second with 13.5% (US$33.3 billion), and the New York Stock Exchange (NYSE) placed only third with 10% (US$24.5 billion).

For more details see Ernst & Young *Globalization – Global IPO Trends Report 2007* at:
www2.eycom.ch/publications/items/2007_global_ipo_trends_report/ey_200 7_global_ipo_trends_report.pdf

This is due to varied factors, including the Sarbanes-Oxley related costs, which emerged after the post-dot.com bubble scandals, IPO fees and the reduced competitiveness of some of the U.S. exchanges still based on obsolete and cost-inefficient trading venues. However, things are evolving. In fact, competition has brought a number of exchanges to react and demutualize, becoming publicly traded for-profit corporations. In addition, the SEC is posing regulatory challenges to modernize U.S. markets and electronic trading is inducing floor-based securities exchanges to modify their trading and business model to meet investors' expectations. In fact, only electronic trading platforms can provide fast, anonymous, cost-effective and efficient execution of trades.

In summary, it is my opinion that competition to provide high speed, high volume, anonymous, reliable, algorithmic trading at lower costs will continue to foster the exchanges consolidation, which in 2006 accelerated with the announcement of the CME-CBOT and the NYSE-Euronext mergers.

Another issue is the enhancement of the current Self Regulatory Organization (SRO) system, which could lead to a single independent regulator with no business ties to the exchanges, thus increasing competition again.

NYSE – New York Stock Exchange

The NYSE was founded in 1792, when 24 brokers and merchants signed the historic *Buttonwood Agreement* to trade securities on a commission basis (see http://en.wikipedia.org/wiki/Buttonwood_Agreement). The organization drafted its constitution on March 8, 1817, and named itself the New York Stock & Exchange Board. In 1863, the name was modified as we know it today to New York Stock Exchange. The NYSE Group, Inc. operates two securities exchanges, the New York Stock Exchange (NYSE) and NYSE Arca (formerly known as the Archipelago Exchange, or ArcaEx, and the Pacific Exchange). On June 1, 2006, NYSE Group, Inc. (NYSE: NYX) and Euronext N.V. announced an agreement to merge the two exchanges on an equal basis.

NYSE Euronext, the holding company created by the combination of NYSE Group, Inc. and Euronext N.V., was launched on April 4, 2007.

On January 17, 2008, NYSE Euronext entered into a definitive agreement to acquire the American Stock Exchange (AMEX). It operates the world's largest and most liquid exchange group, bringing together six cash equities exchanges in five countries and six derivatives exchanges. History of the NYSE can be read at: www.nyse.com/about/history/timeline_chronology_index.html. *A Guide to the NYSE Marketplace* (www.nyse.com/pdfs/nyse_bluebook.pdf) is a very useful resource to learn about the NYSE.

The NYSE provides a liquid and efficient marketplace for stock and other securities of listed companies. On December 31, 2006, the NYSE's global market capitalization was $25 trillion with more than 2,764 issuers – 451 of which are from outside the U.S. In 2006, the average trading day volume was almost 2.3 billion shares, valued at over $86.8 billion. You can read the facts and figures of the NYSE at: www.nysedata.com/nysedata/Default.aspx?tabid=115

NYSE Arca operates an open, all-electronic stock exchange and allows trading of exchange-traded funds, exchange-listed securities and equity options. The trading platform provides customers with direct and anonymous market access.

Companies must meet strict financial and regulatory criteria to be listed. Companies can list as initial public offerings (IPOs) or they can transfer from other markets. Non-U.S. companies can also be cross-listed at foreign exchanges. Securities traded at NYSE or NYSE Arca follow the rules set by the SEC and NYSE Regulation Inc., the independent subsidiary that regulates the NYSE and NYSE Arca markets.

The NYSE represents a mix of electronic trading features and traditional, open-outcry, auction market trading. The order flow, however, comes mainly from floor trading. Approved NYSE broker-dealer entities have trading licenses. Most of them can be either floor brokers or specialists. Floor brokers represent clients' orders with the aim of getting the best price for them, handling trades on behalf of their clients. There are two types of floor brokers. House brokers are employed by brokerage firms and act as agents for their customers and independent brokers are mainly direct-access brokers, who deal at low commission rates.

Specialists act as the contact point between brokers with orders to buy shares and brokers with orders to sell shares. The specialist manages the auction process of a specific stock. He is aware of buy and sell orders entered in his book by the brokers and, in order to ensure an orderly market, he can also commit his firm's capital and act as a buyer or seller.

To read some basic information about the difference between specialists and market makers you can visit the *Investopedia* website at:
www.investopedia.com/ask/answers/128.asp

The Hybrid Market improves process efficiency, automating brokers' and specialists' functions by increasing functionalities and access to liquidity. It is based on a market model that integrates the auction market with automated trading, ensuring speed and certainty of execution. The implementation of advanced technology reduced significantly the average trade-execution time to sub-second turnaround times.

The Exchange declares to have the capacity to trade up to 10 billion shares a day (the record was printed on June 24, 2005, with 3.1 billion shares traded).

The rollout of the Hybrid functionality began in 2006. It meets the requirement to satisfy better-priced quotes in other markets before filling orders in their own market as per the Order Protection Rule of Reg. NMS.

The market supports a number of systems:

- The **SuperDOT** (Designated Order Turnaround System) is an electronic order-routing system, used to send orders to the specialist at the trading post. After the execution of an order, the system sends the report of the transaction to member firms where the order was originated. The great majority of orders pass through SuperDot.

- The **BBSS** (Broker Booth Support System) is an order management system supporting electronic order processing and reporting used by floor brokers to receive orders on the trading floor. The system is connected to the specialist's post and the broker's handheld computer.

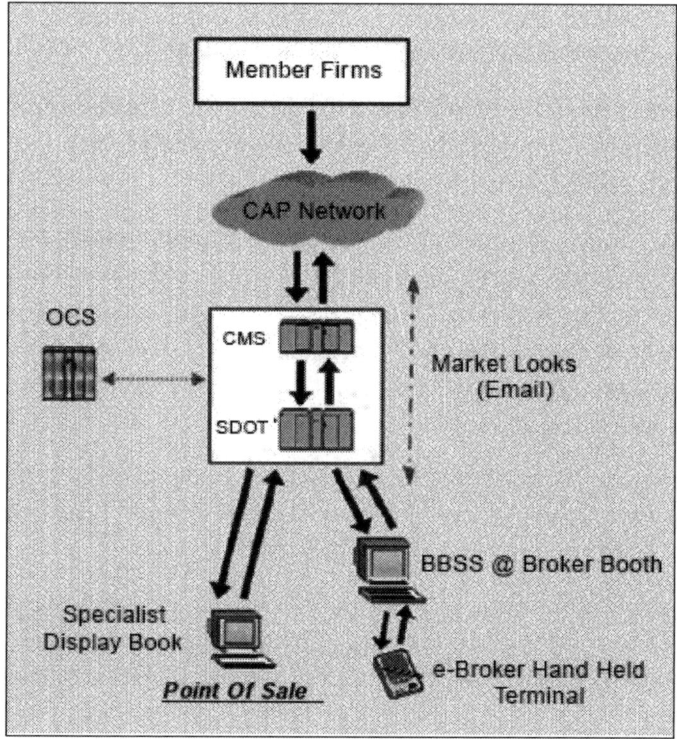

NYSE Strategic tools for order management

- The **NYSE e-Broker** is a wireless handheld order-management tool used to extend order-management capabilities to the broker at the point of sale. The e-Broker connects the firm desk, the broker booth on the floor and the broker in the crowd. It manages quotes and orders and tracks executions.

- **NYSE Direct+** is an electronic connection to the point of sale. It is designed to manage orders that require speed of execution. It enables member firms to enter orders for immediate execution against the NYSE quote. In 2006 it handled about 17% of the volume. Direct+ is the foundation of the Hybrid Market. The NYSE increased the functionality of the platform lifting size and interval restrictions.

Within the Hybrid Market the restrictions of a maximum order size of 1,099 shares and a minimum reload time of 30 seconds was removed, allowing customers to auto-execute up to 1 million shares, sweep the best bid/offer, and trade without time restrictions. These features comply with the requirement set by the Regulation NMS Order Protection Rule to satisfy better quotes in other markets before filling orders in their own markets.

In May 2007, the NYSE Group introduced a new corporate bond trading platform designed to replace the Automated Bond System® or ABS. The new trading platform, which uses an all-electronic trading design, will include the corporate bonds of all NYSE-listed companies and their subsidiaries. This will allow investors to access nearly 5-6,000 bonds in the future (www.nyse.com/pdfs/4043_bonds_brochure.pdf).

Reference:

www.nyse.com

NASDAQ – National Association of Securities Dealers Automated Quotations

The NASDAQ is traditionally home to tech companies' stocks, including communications, media and biotechnology. It is the largest electronic equity securities market in the U.S.

The NASDAQ was founded in 1971, as a wholly owned subsidiary of the National Association of Securities Dealers (NASD), a body with the task to regulate over-the-counter market brokers and dealers. In July 2007, the Financial Industry Regulatory Authority (FINRA) was created through the consolidation of NASD and the member regulation, enforcement and arbitration functions of the NYSE. FINRA is the largest non-governmental regulator for all securities firms doing business in the U.S. (www.finra.org).

NASD divested itself of the exchange between 2000 and 2001 through a two-phase private placement of securities. Securities were offered in private placements to NASD members, some issuers listed on the NASDAQ Stock Market and investment companies. As part of the restructuring plan, on November 9, 2000, it applied with the SEC for registration as a national securities exchange. The NASDAQ Stock Market eventually became operational as an exchange in NASDAQ-listed securities on August 1, 2006 and in other exchange-listed securities in October of the same year. As a result, NASDAQ is now operating as an independent self-regulatory organization.

It is owned and operated by The NASDAQ Stock Market, Inc. (NDAQ), which was listed in 2002. It also operates The NASDAQ Market Center.

The requirement to ensure transparency and fair access in the over-the-counter (OTC) market led NASDAQ, over the years, to implement trading platforms such as the Small Order Execution System (SOES), SuperSOES, SelectNet and SuperMontage.

Today, NASDAQ's platform is the Market Center, which provides access to orders and quotes in national stock exchanges and is also a venue for exchange-traded funds, such as the QQQQ, tracking the NASDAQ-100 index, and other exchange-traded funds (ETFs) listed on the AMEX. With more than 3,200 companies, total volume matched on NASDAQ totaled 123.4 billion shares in the fourth quarter of 2007.

The NASDAQ Stock Market has various tiers of listed companies:

- The **NASDAQ Global Market Companies**, which includes 1450 companies that have applied for listing

- The **NASDAQ Capital Market Companies** (previously called The NASDAQ Small Cap Market), which includes more than 550 companies that have applied for listing

- The **NASDAQ Global Select Market Companies**, with the highest initial listing standards in the world and approximately 1,200 companies listed

Following the SEC's Order Handling Rules of 1996, which favored the growth of electronic communication networks (ECNs), the NASDAQ has acted as a main player in the subsequent consolidation process.

In September 2004, the company acquired Brut, LLC and affiliated entities, the owner and operator of the Brut ECN, from SunGard Data Systems Inc.

On December 8, 2005, NASDAQ acquired Norway Acquisition Corp., formerly known as Instinet Group Incorporated, which owned INET Holding Company, Inc. (owner of INET ATS, Inc., and Island Execution Services, LLC). On February 1, 2006, INET was merged with the Brut broker-dealer, member of the NYSE. However, INET services, such as the trading platform and data dissemination remained separate from the Brut services.

The NASDAQ execution systems were the NASDAQ Market Center (formerly known as Supermontage), the Brut ECN, and the INET ECN. The systems were all linked, but each complying with independent rules.

NASDAQ then initiated the systems' integration into a single matching system (the Integrated System), which was completed on October 30, 2006, for NASDAQ-listed securities. On November 20, 2006, the integration of Brut and INET for trading non-NASDAQ-listed stocks was completed.

The platform links a number of market makers, who are required to post their bid and offer prices into The NASDAQ Market Center, and offers an integrated environment for display, order execution and trade reporting, ensuring anonymity to participants. It allows trading of NASDAQ, NYSE, and AMEX-listed securities on one seamless platform. NASDAQ-listed securities also trade through other markets, such as NYSE, AMEX, ECNs, and regional exchanges, including the Chicago Stock Exchange, the Boston Stock Exchange and the National Exchange.

Competition for volume is high. Broker-dealers are able to view liquidity across different venues, routing orders to get the best price. For example, in January 2008, the Total Market Share in NYSE securities executed on the NASDAQ Market Center was 37.7% (www.nasdaqtrader.com/Trader.aspx?id=MarketShare)

Opening Cross and Closing Cross electronic auctions allow execution of all shares for each stock at a single price. The crosses provide opening and closing prices that are used by Russell Indexes, Standard & Poor's and Dow Jones.

The NASDAQ Market Center ensures connectivity through third-party networks, reducing costs and allowing scalability. Market participants are responsible for maintaining connectivity, mainly by connecting through a third-party extranet provider.

In May 2007, NASDAQ Stock Market Inc. agreed to buy Sweden's OMX AB for 25.1 billion Swedish kronor ($3.7 billion), pushing into Europe after two failed attempts to acquire London Stock Exchange Group Plc. In October 2007 the NASDAQ Stock Market Inc. announced that it entered into a definitive agreement to acquire the Boston Stock Exchange (BSE) and in November 2007 the Philadelphia Stock Exchange (PHLX).

You can find the Annual Reports of the NASDAQ at:
http://ir.nasdaq.com/annuals.cfm.

Reference:

www.nasdaq.com

AMEX – American Stock Exchange

The American Stock Exchange was founded in 1842. At the time it was called the New York Curb Exchange because trading was conducted by the curb on Broad Street, right by the NYSE, then called the New York Stock & Exchange Board. The exchange developed in the context of the California Gold Rush of 1849. It became more established in 1921 when it moved to a building at Trinity Place in New York City. It changed its name to the American Stock Exchange in 1953. NASD purchased AMEX in 1998, but divested of it, transferring control back to the AMEX Membership on January 3, 2005. On January 17, 2008, AMEX agreed to be acquired by NYSE Euronext.

Over the years, the AMEX has played a different role than the NYSE, specializing in small and dynamic companies. The AMEX also supports trading in equity options, but it is best known for its role in starting to list the ETFs back in 1993. AMEX listed 222 ETFs as of December 31, 2006, with 92 new ETFs introduced during the year.

At the AMEX there is a total number of 1433 issues listed. 160 Indexes and 39 new indexes were added only in 2005. In 2006, the AMEX had a total of 197,045,745 options contracts traded, with an average daily volume of 785,043. In equity options trades, the AMEX traded 186,995,065 contracts and an average daily volume of 745,000.

The AMEX is also active in the structured products and the closed-end fund business with 394 and 149 issues listed, respectively.

The AMEX 2006 Annual Report can be found at:
www.amex.com/atamex/annualReview/annual_review_2006.pdf

A very interesting service provided by AMEX is the free Annual Reports Service sponsored by hundreds of companies to improve their visibility and transparency (http://amex.ar.wilink.com/asp/AMX1_search_ENG.asp).

Competition is pushing the exchange to implement technological innovations to respond to regulatory, cost and efficiency requirements. AMEX, in fact, is a specialist-manned, floor-based auction market but it is moving towards implementing electronic functionalities through a new hybrid market structure.

The AMEX marketplace integrates automated execution and floor-based auction trading. A technology upgrade is ongoing based on the new trading platform called AEMI (Auction & Electronic Market Integration), which meets the requirements of the Regulation NMS Order Protection Rule. In fact, it enables the exchange to offer the best bid and offer quotes on AMEX and non-AMEX listed issues. It provides access to automated execution of electronic orders, as well as auction market capabilities when order imbalances require additional liquidity, or when price improvement from the auction process is desired. The rollout of the AEMI trading platform started on November 6, 2006. AEMI primarily supports equity products and ETFs. Options are expected to move to the AEMI. AEMI, in fact, will be integrated with ANTE (AMEX New Trading Environment), the options trading platform of the AMEX.

In 2004, AMEX launched ANTE, an options platform that also supports the hybrid model, combining electronic trading and the floor-based auction process. ANTE replaced previous options trading technology available at the AMEX.

The migration of the platform has increased the system capacity significantly, reducing the order latency and turnaround times.

The following technology also supports professionals at the exchange:

- **BARS** (Booth Automated Routing System) supports order flow management and directs orders straight to floor brokers' handless devices

- **NETS** (New Equity Trading System) is a specialist display book that provides automated order update and order matching

Information about the AMEX systems can be found at:
www.amex.com/amextrader/?href=/amextrader/sysInfo/AEMI/sysInfo_AE MI.html

Reference:

www.amex.com

Futures exchanges have their roots in the 19th century with the establishment of the Chicago Board of Trade, the Kansas City Board of Trade and the precursor of the Chicago Mercantile Exchange. These exchanges were formed because commercial dealers needed to establish a mechanism to partially reduce their unwanted price risk, which hampered the management of their business. Sellers wanted to get rid of price risk associated with owning inventories of corn, grain or butter, and buyers wanted to establish prices for these same products in advance of delivery. In recent years, futures contracts have proliferated on a variety of products, in response to both the need of reducing price risks and speculation.

CBOT – Chicago Board of Trade

The Chicago Board of Trade (CBOT) was established in 1848, when it was founded by 82 Chicago merchants as a grain cash market and is the oldest organized futures exchange. The CBOT was active during the Civil War trading contracts in agricultural commodities including wheat, corn and oats. In 1865, CBOT introduced standardized agreements called futures contracts, introducing the concept of margin.

In 1973, members of the CBOT started the Chicago Board Options Exchange (CBOE). The CBOT successfully launched its first electronic trading system in 1994. In 2000, the CBOT was incorporated as a not-for-profit non-stock corporation and launched a new trading platform, in partnership with the German EUREX.

In the past, the CBOT was based mainly on the open auction system. However, significant steps forward have been made recently to implement electronic trading capabilities. In 2003, the CBOT introduced a new electronic trading platform, powered by LIFFE Connect. In 2004, the exchange partnered with the Chicago Mercantile Exchange, which agreed to clear CBOT products. In 2005, the CBOT announced the demutualization of the Exchange into a for-profit, stock-based holding company and a for-profit, membership exchange subsidiary.

On August 1, 2006, the CBOT launched electronic agricultural futures trading side-by-side with the open auction market during daytime trading hours. Corn, wheat, oats, soybeans, rough rice and ethanol can be traded both on the physical exchange floor and the e-cbot.

Originally, the CBOT traded only agricultural commodities. Over the years, however, new futures contracts were introduced to also include non-agricultural products. In fact today, besides agricultural futures (such as soybeans, wheat, corn, rough rice, ethanol and oats), you can trade futures on interest rates (such as Treasuries, swaps, binary options, Eurodollar), and futures on metals (such as gold and silver).

The CBOT integrates electronic trading with open auction. The trading floor technology provides various capabilities including electronic order-entry to the trading floor, Application Programming Interface (API) connections, electronic order-receipt devices for floor brokers and handheld devices for local traders.

The e-cbot electronic platform, based on the LIFFE Connect trading engine, has an open system that implements an API, allowing users to integrate different types of applications.

During the past two years, the CBOT has been a leader of the ongoing consolidation process of exchanges.

In 2004, an agreement was made to host the agricultural futures and options products of the Kansas City Board of Trade (KCBT) and the Minneapolis Grain Exchange (MGE) on the CBOT electronic platform. An agreement was also made with the Winnipeg Commodity Exchange (WCE) to trade contracts on the CBOT platform.

In 2006, an agreement was reached to host The New York Board of Trade Exchange (NYBOT)'s financial products on the CBOT's electronic trading platform. The CBOT and the Singapore Exchange (SGX) created the Joint Asian Derivatives Exchange (JADE) (www.jadeexchange.com). The futures contracts are traded through the e-cbot platform, powered by LIFFE Connect and cleared by the SGX Derivatives Clearing House.

The most important agreement, however, is related to the merger of the CBOT and the Chicago Mercantile Exchange (CME), which occurred in 2007. The combined company, named CME Group Inc., is traded on the NYSE and NASDAQ under the symbol CME. It has an average daily volume of about 9 million contracts and access to derivatives based on U.S. interest-rate yield curve, equity indexes, foreign exchange, agricultural and industrial commodities, energy, weather and real estate.

You can read more about the merger at:
www.cme.com/files/CMECBOTRevisedFactSheet.pdf

In 2006, the CBOT traded a record 805,884,413 contracts. Exchange average daily volume reached 3,210,695 contracts in 2006, up 20% over 2005. You can find the 2006 Annual Report at:

http://files.shareholder.com/downloads/CME/246016293x0x117302/DB360 F04-4B63-4036-9C3F-CF1CEC571640/81572.pdf

Reference:

www.cbot.com

www.cmegroup.com

CME – Chicago Mercantile Exchange

CME is the largest futures exchange in the U.S. and it owns and operates the largest futures Clearing House.

The predecessor of the Chicago Mercantile Exchange, the Chicago Butter and Egg Board, was formed in 1898 and became the CME in 1919. In 1981, it introduced the CME Eurodollar futures contract, the first contract to be settled in cash. The next year, the CME started to trade the S&P 500 Index futures contract. The first international link between futures exchanges was established in 1984 between the CME and the Singapore Exchange Derivatives Trading Ltd. (SGX). CME Globex, the first global electronic futures trading platform, was introduced in 1992, initially providing only after-hours trading. Today, it offers trading approximately 23 hours a day, five days a week.

The CME launched E-mini S&P 500 futures contracts in 1997, with electronic trading during open-outcry hours for the first time. In June 2002, the CME added onto Globex the e-miNY crude oil and natural gas futures contracts that clear via the New York Mercantile Exchange (NYMEX) clearing house. In November 2003, the CME began providing clearing services to the Chicago Board of Trade (CBOT) for commodity, equity and interest-rate products.

The demutualization of the CME occurred in 2000 by converting the CME membership interests into shares of common stock that can trade separately from exchange trading privileges. At the end of 2001, CME became a wholly owned subsidiary of CME Holdings. Currently, CME is the primary subsidiary of the parent company. In 2002, CME Holdings stock was listed on the NYSE. Class A shares of its common stock began trading on the NYSE under the ticker symbol CME.

To provide you with an idea of the CME dimensions, the exchange traded 1.4 billion contracts in 2006, while the CME Globex volume was 1,015 million contracts.

The 2006 Annual Report is available at: http://files.shareholder.com/downloads/CME/246016293x0x117281/874EA 287-CD91-43FB-9187-83B2463F94F1/2006AR.pdf.

CME products can be traded at the traditional open-outcry trading floors and the Globex electronic trading platform. The open-outcry trading environment still has traders in a trading pit to call out prices and quantities. The open-outcry platform and trading floor systems are linked to Globex. The system allows market participants to introduce their orders regardless of where they are.

The electronic trading environment is complex. It includes order-entry, order-routing, trade-matching and market data components. Applications designed to connect to Globex must conduct a certification process before being enabled in the environment. In 2003, CME introduced new network access alternatives. New telecommunication providers were introduced to provide carrier diversity, higher bandwidth and capacity growth.

CME products fall into five major areas:

1.   Interest rates

2.   Equities

3.   Foreign exchange

4.   Agricultural commodities

5.   Alternative investments

The Clearing House guarantees, clears and settles contracts traded.

The CME has a wide range of products. In fact, you can buy or sell:

- **CME Equity Index** (e.g. the Standard & Poor's 500, NASDAQ-100, Russell 2000)

- **CME Interest Rate** (e.g. the CME Eurodollar futures contract, but also LIBOR futures/options and swap rate futures)

- **CME Foreign Exchange**, such as futures and options on futures on currencies such as the Euro, Japanese yen, British pound, Swiss franc

- **CME Commodity**, such as livestock, dairy and forest products

- **CME Environmental**, such as the weather contracts introduced in 1999

Security futures (stocks, narrow-based indexes and ETFs) are listed and traded on OneChicago, a joint-venture exchange formed in 2002 by CME in partnership with the CBOT and the CBOE. Market participants have access to OneChicago security futures via Globex.

Trading on Globex is possible almost 24 hours a day, from Sunday evening through Friday afternoon. During each session, contracts have pre-defined states. Their timing varies, according to the different products and their specifications. It requires the average trader to know how the market works.

The start of the session occurs in the afternoon and it represents the beginning of the next trading day. Products on Globex are organized as follows:

- **Side-by-Side** contracts trade for a portion of the day simultaneously via open outcry

- **Electronic-Only** contracts trade only electronically

- **After-Hours Electronic** contracts trade electronically after the product stops trading via open outcry

The merger of CBOT and CME into the CME Group will provide significant synergies as the integration of the two exchanges continues.

Reference:

www.cme.com

www.cmegroup.com

KCBT – Kansas City Board of Trade

The Kansas City Board of Trade (KCBT) is a commodity Exchange. At KCBT, you can trade futures and options contracts on hard red winter wheat, for which trade commenced back in 1876, and the Value Line Index, an equally weighted index of about 1,650 stocks.

Trading at KCBT is organized through the traditional open-outcry environment as far as wheat futures and options are concerned, and an electronic trading platform for Value Line and electronic wheat futures.

The Kansas City Board of Trade was founded in 1856 by a group of merchants, but it was only formally organized in 1876. At the beginning, trading was primarily in cash grains. In September 2006, the exchange traded almost 4 million wheat futures contracts. Most of the wheat contracts traded are commercially based. Options on wheat futures were introduced in 1984.

In addition to the traditional wheat products, the KCBT introduced the Value Line futures back in 1982 and options based on the Value Line in 1992. In 2004, the Exchange started implementing modern technology to electronically trade the Value Line and wheat after hours. The CBOT started to host the KCBT futures and options contracts on e-cbot. The KCBT wheat futures and options contracts continue to be traded by open outcry during regular trading hours. Under the hosting agreements, the KCBT market remained independent and maintained separate open and close times. Starting on January 13, 2008, KCBT electronically traded products became available on CME Globex.

The exchange is composed of the Kansas City Board of Trade, the Kansas City Board of Trade Clearing Corp., a wholly owned subsidiary, and the Board of Trade Investment Co.

The Kansas City Board of Trade oversees trading at the Exchange. The Investment Co., of which the Board of Trade owns 51%, manages the building where the exchange is located. The Clearing Corp., established in 1913, acts as a third party to all futures and options transactions.

Reference:

www.kcbt.com

NYMEX – The New York Mercantile Exchange

The New York Mercantile Exchange was founded in 1872 by a group of dairy merchants. Today, the NYMEX is a commodity futures exchange, listing energy and precious metals futures contracts. The Exchange is organized into two divisions, the NYMEX, where you can trade energy, platinum, and palladium, and the Commodity Exchange (COMEX), where you can trade other metals.

On the NYMEX Division you can trade financial instruments related to heating oil, gasoline, crude oil, electricity, natural gas, and propane. You can find, in fact, futures and options contracts, calendar spreads, etc.

On the COMEX Division you can trade gold, silver, copper, and aluminum futures and options. The Exchange clearing house acts as the counterpart to the trades executed.

MiNY futures are also listed at NYMEX and COMEX. They are fractional versions of the crude oil, natural gas, heating oil, gasoline, gold, copper, and silver futures contracts. They trade on the CME Globex electronic trading platform and clear through the NYMEX clearing house.

The Exchange futures and options products can be traded on three different venues:

- Daily open-outcry trading. About 85% of volume is transacted during the four-and-a-half to five hours that the floor is open

- CME Globex

- NYMEX ClearPort electronic platform

ClearPort is an internet-based system that provides access to trading and clearing services. Natural gas, crude oil, petroleum products, freight futures, emissions futures, electricity and coal markets are available on ClearPort.

Energy and metals futures contracts can be traded also on the internet-based NYMEX ACCESS, an electronic order-entry and trade-matching system, when the trading floor is closed.

The Exchange has developed the NYMEX Electronic Order Network (NEON), an API that enables the connection to connect to the Exchange using applications from independent software vendors (ISVs). The API can be added also to proprietary front-end trading system software.

In 2006, the average daily volume rose 38% to 1.2 million contracts and NYMEX launched more than 100 new products.

You can find the 2006 Annual Report at:

http://files.shareholder.com/downloads/NYM/91619742x0x85807/4BFFC03 A-27B8-4E64-925C-317032133304/49582_NymexFinalPDF.pdf.

Reference:
www.nymex.com

NYBOT – The New York Board of Trade Exchange

The New York Board of Trade Exchange started from the New York Cotton Exchange (NYCE), which was founded in 1870, then followed by the Coffee Exchange of the City of New York in 1882. The Coffee Exchange became the Coffee and Sugar Exchange in 1916 and merged with the New York Cocoa Exchange in 1979 to form the Coffee, Sugar & Cocoa Exchange (CSCE).

The NYCE introduced trading on currency futures on its FINEX division back in 1985 and it opened a trading floor in Dublin for FINEX in 1994, adding several currency cross-rate futures contracts.

The CSCE and NYCE formed the Board of Trade of the City of New York as a parent company in 1998. Finally, in 2004 the two exchanges merged to become the NYBOT.

After September 11, 2001, the NYBOT re-located to the back-up facility in Long Island City and moved into a new facility in the World Financial Center two years later.

In January 2007, IntercontinentalExchange (ICE), the electronic energy marketplace, acquired the NYBOT, which became a wholly-owned subsidiary and part of a for-profit, publicly traded corporation.

CBOE – Chicago Board Options Exchange

The Chicago Board Options Exchange started trading options back in 1973 and, in 1975, the Options Clearing Corporation was formed. In 1980 the CBOE and Midwest Stock Exchange consolidated their options markets. In the following years, CBOE launched options on broad-based stock indexes, introducing first the CBOE-100 Index, which was later renamed the S&P 100 Index (OEX), and later options trading on the S&P 500 Index (SPX). In 1990 the CBOE launched the Long-term Equity AnticiPation Securities (LEAPS), which are long-term dated options.

In 1993 the CBOE introduced FLEX options, which allow investors to create certain specifications on options contracts, and VIX, a market volatility index that gauges investor sentiment.

CBOE acquired NYSE options trading business in 1997. It launched CBOEdirect in 2001, the exchange's screen-based trading system initially used for extended-hours trading.

You can read the detailed history of the exchange at: www.cboe.com/AboutCBOE/History.aspx.

The U.S. options markets are linked together on a real-time network and management is provided by the Options Linkage Authority (OLA) – (www.theocc.com/initiatives/ola/ola.jsp).

At this time, OLA consists of:

- The American Stock Exchange (AMEX)

- Boston Options Exchange, Inc. (BOX)

- The Chicago Board Options Exchange (CBOE)

- NYSE Arca

- The Philadelphia Stock Exchange (PHLX)

- The International Securities Exchange (ISE)

In 2005, CBOE developed a physically remote disaster-recovery site setting up a back-up trading facility.

CBOE Hybrid made its debut in 2003 and is a composite of the screen-based and floor-based trading environments.

CBOE Hybrid implements CBOEdirect, a trade engine that provides point & click execution, access to the order book, and the opportunity for price improvement in the open-outcry arena.

Trading desks are offered the HyTS terminal, which provides point & click electronic access to the CBOE market, and order-routing capabilities to other exchanges.

Price improvement is available through AIM (Automated Improvement Mechanism) and COA (Complex Order Auction). AIM provides an automated process for paired orders of any origin type, while the Complex Order Book (COB) and the COA automate the order handling and execution process for complex orders, while continuing to provide the potential for price improvement through a brief auction process.

It appears that large traders still prefer open outcry, where trades are negotiated in an auction among liquidity providers. Last year, 92% of the orders traded on the Hybrid Trading System were executed electronically, accounting for 55% of the volume in those classes. The remaining 8% of orders and 45% of the volume were managed through open outcry.

CBOE through Application Program Interfaces (APIs) allows access to the CBOEdirect.

Many (ISV) have developed an interface to provide firms and member organizations with trading tools that have access to CBOE Hybrid.

The CBOE launched the electronic CBOE Futures Exchange (CFE), which runs on the CBOEdirect platform, in March 2004. The CFE started trading the VIX contracts and several other new related products (www.cfe.cboe.com).

The CBOE partnered to launch the CBOE Stock Exchange, LLC (CBSX) (www.cbsx.com). It is a fully electronic market that is Reg NMS-compliant and offers a price-time matching algorithm. CBSX was launched on March 5, 2007, with the aim to list 2,800 of the most-actively traded NYSE, NASDAQ, and AMEX-listed securities. It is based on the CBOEdirect trading platform.

The CBOE Annual Reports can be found at: www.cboe.com/AboutCBOE/AnnualReports.aspx.

At the end of 2006, the CBOE was able to handle options on more than 1900 individual equities, 28 broad- and sector-based indexes and 96 ETFs.

Trading volume rose to the record 674.7 million contracts. For the year, average daily volume weighed in at nearly 2.7 million contracts. Trading in equity options at CBOE totaled 390.7 million contracts, a rise of 42% over 2005.

In February 2007, the Exchange filed a Registration Statement with the Securities and Exchange Commission (SEC), which details the terms of CBOE's proposed demutualization. CBOE will become a wholly owned subsidiary of a new holding company, CBOE Holdings, Inc.

Reference:

www.cboe.com

OneChicago

OneChicago is a joint venture exchange owned by the CBOE, CME and the CBOT. It offers all-electronic trading of single stock futures, ETF futures and narrow-based indexes. As of today, you can trade these products only at OneChicago in the U.S. Its competitor, NQLX, a joint-venture between NASDAQ and Euronext, ended operations at the end of 2004.

OneChicago was founded in November 2002. The introduction of single-stock futures has been possible thanks to the Commodity Futures Modernization Act of 2000 (CFMA), who clarified oversight of regulation responsibilities. Before then, single-stock and narrow-index futures were not allowed in the U.S. because they involved both securities and futures, causing uncertainties over the regulation responsibilities of the Securities and Exchange Commission (SEC) and the Commodity Futures Trading Commission (CFTC).

At the end of 2006, OneChicago listed 482 futures on single stocks, 5 ETFs and 7 OneChicago Select Indexes, a series of narrow-based security index futures. Trading volume at OneChicago at the close of 2006 totalled 7,923,499 security futures contracts, a 43% increase over 2005.

OneChicago uses a market-maker system based on a number of Lead Market Makers (LMMs). These LMMs are selected based on specific criteria, while other market makers contribute additional liquidity.

Trades executed at OneChicago are cleared and settled by The Options Clearing Corporation (www.optionsclearing.com) or by Chicago Mercantile Exchange Inc. (www.cme.com).

The technology is based on the fully electronic CBOEdirect match engine. Traders can have access to OneChicago from CBOEdirect or Globex. For an overview of the technology implemented at OneChicago see: http://onechicago.com/050000_techno_ops/oc_050000.html.

Reference:

www.onechicago.com

MGEX – Minneapolis Grain Exchange

The exchange was founded as the Minneapolis Chamber of Commerce in 1881 and was mainly a cash market for hard red spring wheat, oats and corn. Only two years later, it introduced the futures contract on hard red spring wheat. In 1947 it was called the Minneapolis Grain Exchange (MGEX).

Index futures and options contracts are available at MGEX on hard red spring wheat, hard red winter wheat, soft red winter wheat, corn and soybeans.

MGEX offers the traditional open-outcry environment, together with electronic contracts on the e-cbot platform. In fact, hard red spring wheat trades electronically after hours. In December 2004, MGEX launched five electronically traded agricultural index contracts. In August 2006, the Exchange started side-by-side electronic and open-outcry trading on spring wheat.

The MGEX is active in both the cash and futures marketplaces. In 2006 the MGEX volume closed the year with a total of 1,655,034 futures and options contracts traded. The cash market at the MGEX is also active with a daily volume average of 1 million bushels of corn, wheat, barley, oats, rye, flax and soybeans.

Starting on January 13, 2008, MGEX electronically traded products became available on CME Globex.

Reference:

www.mgex.com

ISE – International Securities Exchange

Based in New York, the International Securities Exchange (ISE) launched an electronic options exchange in May 2000. To better compete and expand its business, ISE adopted in September 2006 a new holding company structure with the formation of a parent company, ISE Holdings. At ISE you can trade equity and index options.

ISE contributed to the competition in the options markets, as the electronic trading model and platform allowed the exchange to increase efficiency.

Volume in 2006 totaled 592 million contracts, a 31.9% increase compared with 2005. You can find ISE 2006 Annual Report at:

http://www.isestock.com/assets/files/investors/annual_reports/2006_ISE_An nual.pdf.

Members have direct access to the trading system and orders are executed by price priority.

On March 9, 2005, ISE offered its shares in an initial public offering and the shares were traded on the NYSE.

The ISE Stock Exchange launched in December 2006 and trades approximately 6000 products on a fully electronic platform.

It is an electronic marketplace and it provides two capabilities in one platform:

- The **MidPoint Match** is an exchange-based non-displayed market, used to trade equities instantaneously at the exact midpoint price of the National Best Bid and Offer (NBBO)

- **Displayed market** is a fully-electronic displayed market of the Best Bid and Offer trading the common stocks and ETFs listed on the NYSE, NASDAQ, and AMEX

In 2006 ISE entered the Alternative Markets business with the acquisition of the intellectual property and related assets of Longitude, Inc. ISE Alternative Markets will be launched in 2008 and will offer an events market trading platform for derivatives auctions.

Eurex completed the acquisition of ISE on December 19, 2007, and ISE was delisted by NYSE. The transaction created the largest transatlantic derivatives marketplace with significant USD and Euro product coverage, and with significant operations and revenues in both the U.S. and Europe.

References:

www.iseoptions.com

www.isestock.com

ICE – IntercontinentalExchange

The IntercontinentalExchange was established in May 2000. Its shareholders represent very large energy traders.

In June 2001, ICE acquired the currently called ICE Futures, which operated a European energy futures exchange. In 2005, the ICE energy futures were traded on a fully electronic platform. In January 2007, ICE acquired NYBOT and added NYBOT's agricultural products to its electronic platform.

ICE operates a global, electronic marketplace for trading futures and over-the-counter energy contracts, and the leading soft commodity exchange (NYBOT).

ICE provides access to contracts based on crude oil and refined products, natural gas, power and emissions, as well as soft commodities. It conducts the energy futures business through its U.K. subsidiary, ICE Futures.

ICE Futures U.S. provides futures and options markets for agricultural commodities such as cocoa, coffee, cotton, frozen concentrated orange juice, and sugar. The exchange also provides a marketplace for currency cross-rates, the Russell Equity Indexes, the NYSE Commodity Index, the Reuters Jefferies CRB Index, and the US Dollar Index, together with Ethanol and Pulp.

ICE Futures U.S. is also a developer of technology, such as the eCOPS platform (https://ecops.nybot.com/gateway/pages/pub/about.jsp) and NYBOTlive (www.nybotlive.com).

Headquartered in Atlanta, ICE has offices in Calgary, Chicago, Houston, London, New York and Singapore.

References:

www.theice.com

Other markets: regional exchanges, bulletin board stocks, ECN trading

Regional Exchanges

The regional exchanges are organized national securities exchanges registered with the SEC. They include the Boston, Chicago, National, Pacific, and Philadelphia stock exchanges. Regional exchanges list only regional issues and also stocks that list on the regional and the national exchanges. In the past, they were trading mainly local companies. NYSE, AMEX and

NASDAQ listed companies provide a wider market for regional exchanges. The regional exchanges base their business on stocks of NYSE and AMEX-listed companies, which they trade pursuant to grants of Unlisted Trading Privileges (UTPs), which are rights that give an exchange the ability to trade an unlisted security. The OTC/UTP Plan (www.utpdata.com) governs the collection, processing and distribution of all OTC/UTP data. The exchange files an application with the SEC for approval to obtain unlisted trading privileges. The migration to electronic trading and clearing systems helps the exchanges remain competitive. The regional exchanges are linked with the primary markets in UTP issues.

The Consolidated Tape Association (CTA) oversees the dissemination of real-time trade and quote information in NYSE and AMEX listed securities. There are two plans:

- **Consolidated Tape Plan** – which governs trades

- **Consolidated Quotation Plan** – which governs quotes

Through the Consolidated Quotation System (CQS) and the Consolidated Tape System, data streams are produced and distributed (www.nysedata.com/cta).

Currently, the participants are:

- American Stock Exchange

- Boston Stock Exchange

- Chicago Board Options Exchange

- Chicago Stock Exchange

- Financial Industry Regulatory Authority

- International Securities Exchange

- NASDAQ Stock Market

- National Stock Exchange

- New York Stock Exchange

- NYSE Arca

- Philadelphia Stock Exchange

Although the regional exchanges may not represent significant quote competitors, they provide competition based on low cost and new products.

CHX – Chicago Stock Exchange

The Chicago Stock Exchange (CHX) was founded in 1882. In 1920, the CHX Stock Clearing Corporation was established. CHX merged with the exchanges in St. Louis, Cleveland and Minneapolis/St. Paul to form the Midwest Stock Exchange in 1949. In 1959, the New Orleans Stock Exchange became part of the Midwest Stock Exchange.

In 1993, the exchange changed its name back to Chicago Stock Exchange. The history of the CHX can be read at:
www.chx.com/content/Inside_CHX/Gen_History.html.

The CHX is an equity exchange and is a self-regulatory organization, which operates with the oversight of the SEC.

In February 2005 the SEC approved the ownership structure change from a not-for-profit, member–owned company (members had an ownership interest and the privilege to trade on the floor) to a for-profit stock-holder owned corporation. The exchange became a Delaware stock corporation, operating as a direct and wholly owned subsidiary of CHX Holdings, Inc.

CHX is part of the National Market System in competition with all U.S. equity markets. It is possible to access the Exchange trading systems and other marketplaces linked through inter-market connections. The SEC rules also allow the trade of stocks listed on other exchanges.

The exchange has completed its transition to the New Trading Model. On December 7, 2006, the CHX announced the launch of its automated trading system. Participants can submit orders for display, execution and cancellation from any location.

The stocks that can be traded through the CHX Matching System include NYSE, AMEX, regional and NASDAQ-listed securities. The Matching System operates a regular trading session and an after-hours session.

Participants send orders to the Matching System by using specific protocols on different types of connections. The Order Management System (OMS) validates and routes orders. The matching engine compares the order's price with limit orders in the book. The order is executed if it can be matched at a price within the NBBO. Otherwise, it will be placed on the book or rejected.

BrokerPlex, the institutional order-management system, has been upgraded. Orders are routed to a CHX Institutional Broker using BrokerPlex, which allows the broker to interact with the Matching System and to obtain executions from other marketplaces.

The Exchange incurred losses of $4,771,000 and $3,338,000 during the years ended December 31, 2005, and 2006, respectively. In 2005, the average daily volume was 55,523,669 compared with 76,230,373 printed in 2004.

The 2006 Annual Report can be found at:
www.chx.com/content/CHX_Holdings/DownloadableDocs/1_AnnualReport
s/CHX_Holdings_2006.pdf.

Reference:

www.chx.com

BSE – Boston Stock Exchange

The Boston Stock Exchange was founded in 1834. Initially, only stocks of local banks and insurance companies were traded on the exchange. Later, railroad, utility, and other stocks were listed.

You can read the Annual Reports at:
http://www.bostonstock.com/About/AnnualReports.aspx.

In November 2006, the BSE, together with Citigroup, Credit Suisse, Fidelity Brokerage Company, Lehman Brothers and Merrill Lynch, launched an electronic stock exchange in a Reg NMS environment, the Boston Equities Exchange (BeX), accepting orders/trades in more than 8400 NYSE-listed, NASDAQ, AMEX, ETFs, and BSE sole-listed instruments.

BeX's technology is based on technology from Atos-Euronext and Lava Trading. The fully automated system can support trading of equities, options and futures. Orders are handled on a strict price and time priority and trades must be at or better than the NBBO.

The BSE, with its partners Bourse de Montréal Inc. and Interactive Brokers Group LLC, formed the Boston Options Exchange Group LLC (BOX). The exchange operates as an automated equity options market on U.S. equities, equity indices, ETFs, and single stock futures. BOX started operations back in February 2004 and as of June 2006 listed 478 issues to reach up to 1,000 issues by the end of 2006.

BOX introduced the price-improvement period or PIP (see www.bostonoptions.com/pric/pri.php for the details), which is an auction that allows brokers to improve the price of their orders above the NBBO.

Options traded on BOX are cleared by the Options Clearing Corporation (OCC). BOX options are fungible with options traded on any other exchange. Contract specifications of listed options are the same as options traded at other exchanges.

BOX does not have a specialist system. Multiple marketmakers, which are qualified participants, compete for orders, ensuring liquidity. Only broker dealers registered in the U.S. may become BOX Trading Participants.

Market data is provided to the Options Price Reporting Authority (OPRA) and is available through data vendors.

BOX migrated in July 2006 to a trading engine named SOLA, licensed from the Montreal Exchange (MX). This trading engine is able to support the structure of the exchange and provides an API to interface participants to the trading engine.

On September 5, 2007, the BSE announced that it had discontinued the operations of the BeX because of its inability to gain significant share in the highly competitive market.

In October 2007, The NASDAQ Stock Market Inc. announced that it entered into a definitive agreement to acquire the BSE for about $61 million.

In December 2007, the BSE announced that it had reached an agreement to sell its ownership position in BOX to the MX, subject to regulatory approval.

References:

www.bostonstock.com

www.bostonexchange.com

www.bostonoptions.com

PHLX – Philadelphia Stock Exchange

The equity exchange was founded, as the first organized stock exchange in the U.S., in 1790 by merchants and it belonged to the Philadelphia Board of Brokers. Since 1870, it has established a clearing house to settle trades and help delivery. The exchange merged with the Baltimore Stock Exchange in 1949 and with the Washington Stock Exchange in 1953. In 1975, the exchange introduced the small-order-routing and auto-execution system PACE (Philadelphia Automated Communication and Execution). It also started operating on equity options trading. In 1982, the exchange introduced currency options and in 1988 it also introduced the AUTOM (Automated Options Market) system. The exchange changed its structure to a share-based for-profit company in January 2004.

The detailed history of the exchange can be read at: www.phlx.com/exchange/phlxhistory.pdf.

At the exchange you can trade more than 7,000 stocks, more than 2,300 equity options, 15 sector index options, and currency pairs. You can trade HOLDRS (HOLding company Depositary ReceiptS) that allow an investor to own a group of stocks in a single investment according to the industry group or sector, FLEX Options, and Long-term Equity AnticiPation Securities (LEAPS). The PHLX's Gold/Silver Sector, the Oil Service Sector, Semiconductor Sector, PHLX/KBW Bank Index and Utility Sector are popular industry indicators.

The Annual Reports can be found at: www.phlx.com/pub/annualreport.html.

The volume for securities traded on the exchange in 2006 was 789,233,385 shares in equities, 265,370,986 contracts in equity options, 7,625,523 in index options and 131,508 in currency options. In 2007, volume on equity options reached a high of 399,147,901, more than 50% year-over-year growth.

Trading at the PHLX rose 33% in the first quarter of 2007, faster than the whole U.S. options market, as new contracts on currencies geared for retail investors and exchange-traded funds lured investors. In 2006, the exchange started trading futures contracts on interest rates.

The PHLX currently has about a 15% share of all U.S. options trading.

The exchange has the ownership of the Philadelphia Board of Trade (PBOT), the futures market launched in 2006 (www.phlx.com/pbot/index.html).

In addition, PHLX launched the PBOT Market Data Distribution Network in July 2006, aimed to sell market and index data. Options and futures traded at the PHLX and the PBOT clear at the Options Clearing Corporation. PHLX XL is an electronic options-trading system aimed at maximizing liquidity and is able to execute orders of any size.

In November 2006, in advance of Reg NMS's mandated start date, PHLX launched the all-electronic equity trading system, PHLX XLE, leveraging the technology of PHLX XL. It provides a Reg NMS-compliant environment with participants enabled to submit orders anonymously from any location.

The PBOT XL platform can connect traders to a fully electronic PBOT, which was launched to market products and trading instruments that complement existing offers trading in the U.S. and internationally.

On November 7, 2007, NASDAQ announced that it entered into a definitive agreement to acquire PHLX. It will pay $652 million in cash consideration for the capital stock of the PHLX.

Reference:

www.phlx.com

NSX – National Stock Exchange

The National Stock Exchange is an electronic stock exchange conceived with a low-cost structure as an alternative to primary markets. The exchange was founded in 1885 as the Cincinnati Stock Exchange but, in November 2003, the name changed to the National Stock Exchange. The trading floor was replaced with an automated market in 1980.

The exchange has a national presence. It demutualized into a for-profit corporation in 2006. The low-cost structure allows the exchange to compete with primary markets, fulfilling the role of a cost-efficient market for NASDAQ, NYSE and AMEX-listed stocks and ETFs.

The number of U.S. listed ETFs in April 2008 has increased 49% to 740 compared with the previous year. Trading volume of ETFs totaled $1.6 trillion during the same month. The ETF monthly statistics can be found at http://www.nsx.com/marketdata_monthly_etf2.html.

In October 2006, NSX BLADE, the new technology platform, was introduced to offer strict price-time priority, speed, highly competitive exchange pricing and an order-delivery function. NSX BLADE has scalable capacity and connectivity options, helping NSX to provide services to ECNs, algorithmic traders and agency brokers.

Reference:

www.nsx.com

Over-The-Counter (OTC) Markets

The Financial Industry Regulatory Authority (FINRA) regulates broker-dealers that operate in the over-the-counter (OTC) market. On the OTC market you can trade equity securities, corporate bonds, government securities and derivative products. The OTC Bulletin Board (OTCBB) and the Pink Sheets, for example, operate within the OTC market.

The Pink Sheets and the OTCBB are quotation services for OTC securities. The Pink Sheets is a privately owned company. Unlike the OTCBB, issuers do not have to file financial reports to the SEC to be quoted.

OTCBB – The Over-the-Counter Bulletin Board

The OTC Bulletin Board is an electronic inter-dealer quotation system. It transmits real-time quotes, trade prices, and volume for over-the-counter securities not listed on NASDAQ or another national securities exchange. The OTCBB started operations in 1990, with the aim to provide transparency in the OTC market, facilitating the dissemination of quotation and last-sale information as a pilot program. The SEC approved the operation of the OTCBB on a permanent basis only in 1997. The OTCBB does not have listing requirements. To be quoted on the OTCBB, companies must file financial reports with the SEC or with their banking or insurance regulators. The OTCBB provides trading services for U.S. and foreign securities, warrants, American Depositary Receipts (ADRs), and Direct Participation Programs (DPPs).

Investopedia defines a DPP as "a business venture designed to let investors participate directly in the cash-flow and tax benefits of the underlying investment. DPPs are generally passive investments that invest in real estate or energy-related ventures."

The OTCBB allows access to about 3,300 issues and it has more than 230 participating market makers.

In 2007 the average daily share volume was 1,717,191,282, about 30% lower than the record volume printed in 2006.

Market makers cannot start quoting a security whose issuer does not meet filing requirements with the SEC or other regulatory authority. The OTCBB does not provide automated trade executions, but trades in domestic equity issues, Canadian issues and ADRs must be reported within 90 seconds through an automated system called ACT (Automated Confirmation Transaction service).

Note: NASD Notice to Members 93-62 and Rule 6600 reports a detailed explanation of the requirements for reporting OTC equity trades.

In 1999, the SEC approved the OTCBB Eligibility Rule, which required securities not quoted to report their current financial information to meet eligibility requirements. It is important to note that NASDAQ has no relationship with issuers of the OTCBB. Companies have filing or reporting requirements only with the SEC or other regulatory authority. Issuers may contact a market maker for sponsorship of a security, who then apply to quote securities. The OTCBB does not charge issuers with fees for their quotation. Also, market makers are not remunerated to quote issuers' securities.

The OTCBB data is disseminated through market data vendors.

The history of the OTCBB can be read at:
www.otcbb.com/aboutOTCBB/overview.stm#abouthistory.

Reference:

www.otcbb.com

Pink Sheets

Pink Sheets LLC is a privately held company headquartered in New York City. It is an electronic quotation and trading system in the OTC securities market. Pink Sheets is not a SEC registered stock exchange.

Pink Sheets, given its name for the color of paper used, started in 1904. Together with the Yellow Sheets they were a resource for trading OTC stocks and bonds.

Note: Yellow Sheets provides updated bid/ask prices, as well as other information about OTC bonds.

In September 1999, Pink Sheets introduced the Electronic Quotation Service, which provides internet-based, real-time quotes of equities and bonds, and www.pinksheets.com was launched in 2000. For the history of Pink Sheets, see: www.pinksheets.com/about/history.jsp.

The Pink Sheets offers a quotation service for market makers. Broker-dealers who are market makers may apply to quote securities on the Pink Sheets, which does not list securities. There are no listing requirements to be quoted on the Pink Sheets.

To be quoted on the Pink Sheets, issuers need to find a SEC-registered and member of FINRA broker-dealer (market maker) willing to quote the company's stock. Many companies, in fact, do not meet the minimum requirements for trading on a national securities exchange.

Due to costs associated with the Sarbanes-Oxley legislation, some companies have de-listed from exchanges. Others do not print large trading volumes and choose not to spend the money needed to be listed on an exchange.

Pink Sheets in May 2007 introduced new categories for companies traded, providing more transparency to the market. Categories are based on the level of disclosure, quality and timeliness.

Companies with sufficient operating businesses who can provide credible disclosure, qualify for OTCQX (a listing service for issuers of securities that are traded OTC). Detailed information is available at: www.otcqx.com.

OTCQX is designed to meet the expectations of small/medium publicly traded U.S. companies and foreign companies listed on qualified international stock exchanges. About 20% of Pink Sheets/OTCBB companies could qualify to be listed at OTCQX and it allows issuers to publish audited reports.

The www.pinksheets.com site (www.pinksheets.com/pink/otcguide/investors_market_tiers.jsp) reports the various market OTC tiers that include:

- **PremierQX** – U.S. issuers able to meet the financial requirements to list on the NASDAQ's Capital Market

- **PrimeQX** – issuers operating companies with audited financials, but not of sufficient size to be on PremierQX

- **International PremierQX** – international exchange-listed companies of size and quality to meet the financial qualifications of the NYSE Worldwide Listing Standards

- **International PrimeQX** – issuers that have ongoing business operations with audited financials and management review but not of sufficient size to be on International PremierQX

Securities that do not meet the above standards are organized in the following categories:

- Securities quoted solely on the OTCBB

- SEC Current – companies that are SEC reporting and current in their financial reporting and are quoted on both the OTCBB and Pink Sheets

- Adequate Current Information – companies that conform to Pink Sheets guidelines

- Limited Information Available – companies with some information posted in the last six months

- No Information – other Pink Sheets stocks

Trading in Pink Sheets securities was more than $162 billion of dollar volume and 769 billion of share volume in 2007. More than 5,000 OTC securities are electronically traded on the Pink Sheets (see: www.pinksheets.com/pink/about/news.jsp).

For more information on the OTC market, you can read the SEC: Over-the-Counter Markets – OTC Bulletin Board – Pink Sheets at: www.sec.gov/divisions/marketreg/mrotc.shtml.

References:

www.pinksheets.com

www.otcqx.com

ECNs – Electronic Communication Networks

ECNs represent an alternative to traditional market making and floor trading.

At the beginning of their history, ECNs were mainly closed trading systems. Prices on ECNs were better than those posted on NASDAQ and they were not integrated into the national market system, with a negative impact on the average investor. The SEC in 1996 adopted the Order Handling Rules (OHR), which requires market makers and specialists to display customer limit orders that were priced better than a specialist's or OTC market maker's quote.

In 1998, Regulation ATS (www.sec.gov/rules/final/34-40760.txt) gave alternative trading systems the choice to be a market participant and register as a broker-dealer, or to be a separate market and register as an exchange. Subscribers, typically institutional investors, broker-dealers, and marketmakers, can place trades directly. Individual investors, with an account with a broker-dealer subscriber, can have their orders routed to an ECN. Subscribers, typically, use limit orders. ECNs automatically match orders for execution, which are posted on their systems.

To have a better understanding of the SEC view and regulating activities performed, refer to:

Special Study: *Electronic Communication Networks and After-Hours Trading – Division of Market Regulation –* June 2000 at: www.sec.gov/news/studies/ecnafter.htm.

ECNs implement platforms able to support high speed, high volume, anonymous trading. Algorithmic trading, increasingly common in equity markets, is widely applied on these platforms. Today, individuals can trade stocks on ECNs as institutions.

As a result of increasing competition, the past years have seen a fast consolidation process that has involved exchanges and ECNs with costs and technology as the main drivers. This tendency is to continue in the future and is transforming the landscape of exchanges and ECNs.

In April 2005, the NYSE and Archipelago announced a merger agreement that led to the NYSE Group, Inc. Archipelago, which operated the Archipelago Exchange (ArcaEx), was one the first ECNs, along with Instinet, Island and Bloomberg Tradebook. In September 2005, Archipelago acquired PCX Holdings, Inc., the parent company of the Pacific Exchange and PCX Equities, to create an electronic equity and options exchange. Archipelago grew organically and through acquisitions. It completed its merger with Redibook in 2002. Redibook was founded in November 1997 by Spear, Leeds & Kellogg (SLK) and attracted investments from Charles Schwab, Fidelity and other large firms. The acquisition of Globenet allowed ArcaEx (Archipelago Exchange) to also trade OTC Bulletin Board stocks. In March 2006, the merger of the NYSE and Archipelago Holdings was completed. NYSE Group operates the NYSE and NYSE Arca (formerly known as Arca Ex, and the Pacific Exchange).

Island, one of the first ECNs, was supporting market structure reforms and the advantages of auto-execution electronic systems. Eventually, Island was bought by Instinet in September 2002. Instinet merged its own ECN platform with Island's and created Inet. In 2005 NASDAQ announced the acquisition of Inet.

Brut was launched in May 1998. It later merged with Strike Technologies, another ECN. Brut became the second-largest ECN and it was sold in 2004 to NASDAQ. On July 14, 2006, the SEC approved NASDAQ's System Integration proposal. This approval allowed NASDAQ to integrate the NASDAQ Market Center, Brut and Inet into a single platform, which occurred in November 2006.

Tradebook (www.bloombergtradebook.com) is owned by Bloomberg. Established in 1996, it targets the buy-side and provides direct connectivity to 36 markets and access trading capabilities on 65 markets. Tradebook combines brokerage services as well as ECN features.

Nextrade became operational in 1999. It filed to become an electronic stock exchange but never gained market share. In January 2006, Citigroup acquired OnTrade Inc., the broker-dealer that is registered with the Commission, and operated Nextrade.

The Track ECN (www.trackecn.com), headquartered in New York City, is a division of Track Data Securities Corp. and is owned by Track Data Corporation (NASDAQ: TRAC).

Globenet, created in 2001, launched Bullet X, a platform automating the mostly manual OTCBB market. It was bought in 2002 by ArcaEx, which has leveraged its technology for its ArcaEdge OTCBB platform.

MarketXT, first known as Eclipse Trading, was launched in January 2000 as an after-hour ECN and was acquired by Tradescape soon afterwards.

Tradescape's takeover by E*Trade in 2002 did not include the ECN, which subsequently shut down.

In 2005, Knight Capital Group Inc. (www.knight.com) formed a subsidiary called Direct Edge ECN LLC to acquire ATTAIN ECN from Domestic Securities Inc. and certain of its affiliates and shareholders.

DirectEdge is an independent broker-dealer owned by a consortium of three firms: Knight Capital Group, Citadel Derivatives Group, LLC, and The Goldman Sachs Group, Inc. (www.directedge.com/default.aspx). DirectEdge has average daily volumes well over 600 million shares. Starting December 2007, Direct Edge began the process of migrating its public quotations from the Alternative Display Facility to the NSX. On DirectEdge it is possible to trade Tape A (NYSE), Tape B (Regionals), Tape C (NASDAQ) and OTCBB securities.

BATS Trading (Better Alternative Trading System) (www.batstrading.com) was formed in June 2005 to offer direct connectivity to U.S. broker-dealers. Privately held, BATS investors include Citigroup, Credit Suisse, Deutsche Bank, Getco, JPMorgan Chase, Lehman Brothers, Lime Brokerage, Morgan Stanley, Merrill Lynch and Wedbush Morgan.

Based in Kansas City, BATS Trading is able to quote via the ISE Stock Exchange and the NSX.

The ECN, which bases its business on high speed connectivity, has seen an impressive growth since the beginning of its operations. In January 2008, BATS set a daily volume record with more than 1.18 billion shares traded, a 11.3% share of NASDAQ volume and 8% of NYSE. The company reported a sharp volume increase since NASDAQ completed its migration to Single Book and decommissioned SuperMontage and Brut.

Dealer vs. order-driven auction markets, electronic vs. floor trading.

Every market has an execution system to match buyers and sellers. The execution system contributes to define a market structure, making it specific for a given marketplace. Market structure significantly influences traders' behavior. Understanding market structure will, therefore, help you build strategies suited for a specific market, especially when trading very short-term strategies. Often, markets are classified taking into account the different types of execution systems. There are four main types of markets classified using this criteria:

- Quote-driven markets

- Order-driven markets

- Brokered-markets

- Hybrid markets – hybrid markets implement a combination of the other three systems

In quote-driven markets, dealers are involved in every trade. Traders negotiate their trades directly with a dealer or through their broker, who can arrange trades with a dealer. Dealers can trade among themselves, while in pure quote-driven markets traders cannot. Dealers intermediate all trades that occur on the marketplace quoting prices at which they will buy or sell and supplying liquidity to the market. Some markets have inter-dealer brokers that help dealers arrange their trades and allow dealers to trade anonymously. Quote-driven markets are very common. Many bond, currency and stock markets are quote-driven. Most markets have electronic data systems to facilitate communications with and among dealers.

In order-driven markets traders arrange their trades with each other without the dealers' intermediation. Order-driven markets include oral auctions, single-price auctions, continuous rule-based auctions and crossing networks. Order-driven markets arrange trades applying a set of rules to traders' orders. Order precedence rules determine which buyers trade with which sellers. Trade pricing rules determine the price at which the trade is made. In these markets, dealers trade on an equal basis with other traders. Most markets are auction markets. Some markets have single-price auctions; others conduct continuous two-sided auctions in which traders continuously try to arrange their trades; others have crossing networks to match orders at prices taken from other markets. Many markets have electronic order-matching systems, but you can also find markets that conduct oral auctions. As order precedence rules are used in order-driven markets, traders cannot choose with whom they trade. Therefore, markets elaborate rules to prevent settlement failures and ensure that traders are trustworthy and creditworthy. The main futures exchanges, most stock and options exchanges and many trading systems used by ECNs are order-driven.

In brokered markets, brokers match buyers and sellers. In these markets, brokers fulfil the role of finding liquidity. Normally, large blocks of bonds and stocks are traded in brokered markets. For small size trades, liquid markets can ensure to arrange trades at low costs. Brokers play their role when an investor is willing to trade large blocks. In this case, the investor needs to find a suitable counterpart in order not to significantly influence prices. Hybrid markets are a mix of the previously described markets. NYSE and the NASDAQ Stock Market are hybrid markets. The NYSE is an order-driven market, but it requires its specialist dealers to offer liquidity when needed. The NASDAQ Stock Market is a quote-driven market, but it requires its dealers to display and often execute public limit orders. In these markets brokers are also allowed to execute large block trades and provide some characteristics of brokered markets.

During the past years, exchanges have started to bring technology into their trading models and automate their trading systems. However, floor-based trading systems are still common. For example, the NYSE, the CBOT, the CME, and the NYMEX use floor-based trading systems. Traders on the floor use electronic systems to route orders and send confirmations, but they still arrange trades as they did in the past.

Both floor-based and automated trading systems have advantages and disadvantages, suitable for different types of market players. **Automated systems present a low cost and high speed trading environment excellent for small traders to trade active markets.** Here, traders have direct control over their orders without the need of brokerage services and the related costs. Automated electronic markets are scalable, providing significant economies of scale. Many exchanges have already merged to exploit these economies of scale and the process is likely to continue in the future. Electronic trading systems also allow very efficient audit trails. On the other hand, floor-based systems work well for brokers who search for traders to fill their orders or for traders who need to exchange information not easily available in electronic systems. These advantages are typical for large traders, making floor-based markets an ideal environment for large institutional traders. Floor-based markets implement automated systems to support their trading activities. These systems may include limit order books, order-routing systems, reporting systems, etc. Even with all the technology available, these markets remain labor-intensive. In contrast, electronic trading systems do not require large staffs. Therefore, they are cheaper, as they do not require floor brokers and sales brokers. Brokerage clients can access the market without intermediation, allowing a direct access to the market. Brokers guarantee and settle their clients' trades and also provide valuable services to traders.

Products

Generalities

In U.S. markets you can trade an impressive number of financial instruments. Based on your expectations in terms of risk and return, you can approach the instruments that suit you the most. In this chapter, I will describe the main products available for you to trade or invest in as they all have different characteristics. Financial assets represent the ownership of real assets and the cash flows that they produce. For example, stocks and bonds are financial assets. Stockholders own the assets of a company after all creditors have been paid off. Bondholders own the assets of a company that defaults and becomes bankrupt. Issues trade in primary markets when issuers first create and sell them. Following that, trading occurs in secondary markets. Trading in new equity issues takes place in the Initial Public Offering (IPO) market. Issuers request underwriters to help them sell the assets. Underwriters are broker-dealers at investment banks who find buyers for the securities. Derivative contracts are instruments that derive their value from the value of the underlying instruments upon which they are based. Typical derivative contracts are futures, options, forward contracts and swaps. Derivative contracts are by definition in zero net supply and the sum of all long positions minus the sum of all short positions is always zero.

Mutual funds, closed-end funds

A popular way to invest in financial markets is through mutual funds. To give you an idea of the dimension of investments in these instruments, mutual-fund assets worldwide increased 6.2% to an impressive $25.82 trillion at the end of the third quarter of 2007. A mutual fund is a company that invests in a portfolio of securities. Buyers of mutual-fund shares are its shareholders. Funds buy securities with the money provided by their investors, who share the risk and reward. Mutual funds allow investors – also with limited money available to invest – to diversify their portfolio and risk.

There are three basic types of mutual funds. They are stock, bond, and money -market funds. Stock mutual funds invest mainly in shares of stocks issued by U.S. or foreign companies. Bond mutual funds invest primarily in bonds. Money-market mutual funds invest in short-term securities issued by the U.S. government and its agencies, U.S. corporations, and state and local governments.

Stock funds

As a buyer of a stock mutual fund, you are one of the owners of each of the securities in the fund's portfolio. Stocks have historically outperformed other types of investment and, in particular, bonds, printing returns higher than inflation. They should be considered for a long-term investment. Common types of stock funds are:

Strategy:

- **Growth Funds** invest in stocks of fast-growing companies with potential for capital appreciation

- **Income Funds** invest in stocks that pay regular dividends

- **Blend Funds** invest in a mix of both growth and value stocks

Size:

- **Large-cap Funds** invest in well established corporations, which tend to pay dividends and whose market value is large (generally more than 10$ billion)

- **Mid-cap Funds** invest in mid-sized companies whose market value is in the range of $2 billion to $10 billion

- **Small-cap Funds** invest in companies whose market value, is less than $2 billion

Sector funds

Sector funds specialize in a particular industry or segment of the market. Examples of sectors include technology, insurance, retail, banking, biotechnology, and utilities. These funds offer diversification within a particular industry.

Index funds

Index funds aim to achieve the same return of a given market index. For example, they can replicate a stock index, such as the S&P 500 or the NASDAQ. Their characteristic is that the manager does not apply an active strategy. The portfolio of investments, in fact, is weighted in order to mirror the index performance. These funds are a form of passive investing; they are cost-efficient and often outperform actively managed funds.

Bond funds

Bond fund shares represent the ownership in a pool of bonds. When you buy a bond, you lend money to the issuer – a company, municipality, or government agency. The issuer has to repay the face value of the bond at the maturity date and commits to make periodic interest payments. Normally, these funds have low volatility and produce a regular income. Their risk depends on the fluctuation of interest rates and inflation.

The main types of bond funds are:

- U.S. government bond funds

- Municipal bond funds

- Corporate bond funds

U.S. government bond funds invest in debt securities issued by the government and its agencies. Typical debt instruments are:

- Treasury bills

- Treasury notes

- Treasury bonds

- Mortgage-backed securities

Municipal bond funds invest in debt securities issued by state and local governments. Corporate bond funds invest in bonds issued by corporations. They are not backed by any government institution, but the interests paid are higher to compensate risk and lower ratings.

Money-market funds

Money-market funds invest in instruments issued by the U.S. government, U.S. corporations, and state and local governments, which have, typically, short maturity dates of less than 13 months. These funds are appropriate for a short-term investment. Although they are not risk-free, they are indicated if you want to preserve the value of your investment. They are characterized by very low volatility. They have stringent requirements related to credit quality, maturity, and diversification standards to minimize risk.

A **mutual fund** is usually a corporation or a business trust owned by its shareholders and is externally managed. Open-End Investment Company is the legal name for a mutual fund. There is no limit to the number of available shares because the fund company can create new shares to meet investor demand.

A **closed-end fund** is an investment company that sells a fixed number of shares in an IPO that are traded on a secondary market. The price fluctuates based on investors' supply and demand. Closed-end funds are not required to redeem shares and have managed portfolios. The fund is trading at a premium when the share price is more than the net asset value (NAV). It is trading at a discount when the share price is lower than the NAV.

A **Unit Investment Trust** (UIT) issues an initial public offering of a fixed number of redeemable securities (units). It will terminate and dissolve on a specified date. When a trust is dissolved, proceeds from the securities are paid to shareholders. A UIT has an unmanaged portfolio. Like a mutual fund, shares of a UIT can be redeemed on any business day. When this occurs, the UIT or its sponsor may purchase them and offer them to the public.

Mutual funds are regulated by the federal government through the SEC. All funds must provide current and potential investors with a prospectus and a shareholder report. The prospectus describes the fund's goals, fees and expenses, investment strategies, and risks.

Annual and semi-annual shareholder reports present the financial statements and performance. They also report the securities that are held in the fund's portfolio. Investors must also be provided with information about fees, in particular:

- **Maximum Sales Charge** – imposed on purchases to charge for the purchase of shares

- **Maximum Deferred Sales Charge** – maximum charge when shares are redeemed or sold

- **Maximum Sales Charge on Reinvested Dividends** – maximum fee when dividends are reinvested in the purchase of additional shares. Since April 2000, new funds cannot charge this fee.

- **Redemption Fee** – charged when an investor redeems shares

- **Exchange Fee** – charged when an investor transfers money from one fund to another of the same fund family

- **Annual Account Maintenance Fee** – charged, for example, to maintain low-balance accounts

- **Management Fee** – charged for the management of the portfolio of securities and to provide related services

- **Distribution Fee** – charged to pay marketing and advertising expenses.

- **Total Annual Fund Operating Expenses** – the sum of the annual operating costs

An interesting resource is the mutual-fund expense analyzer available at: http://apps.nasd.com/investor_Information/ea/nasd/mfetf.aspx.

An important reference is also:

SEC – Division of Investment Management: Report on Mutual Fund Fees and Expenses, December 2000
www.sec.gov/news/studies/feestudy.htm

A mutual fund is governed by a board of directors. At least 40% of a fund's board of directors must be independent of the fund's investment adviser or principal underwriter. The SEC monitors the compliance with the Investment Company Act of 1940, which imposes restrictions on mutual funds, investment advisers, directors, principal underwriters, officers, and employees of the fund, and other statutes, including the Investment Advisers Act, the Securities Exchange Act of 1934, and the Securities Act of 1933.

As a reference and introduction about mutual funds see:

SEC - Invest Wisely: An Introduction to Mutual Funds

www.sec.gov/investor/pubs/inwsmf.htm
Another resource for information is the site of The Investment Company Institute (ICI), the national association of U.S. investment companies: www.ici.org.

Hedge funds

Hedge funds pool investors' money to invest in financial instruments. Hedge funds are not required to register with the SEC and they are subject to few regulatory controls. Historically, only accredited investors and large institutions could invest in these funds. Hedge funds have often established high initial investment minimums. Typically, they issue securities in private offerings that are not registered with the SEC. Hedge funds are not required to provide periodic reports according to the Securities Exchange Act of 1934. In December 2004, the SEC issued a rule change that required most hedge funds to register with the SEC by February 1, 2006, as investment advisers under the Investment Advisers Act.

The requirement, with minor exceptions, applied to firms managing in excess of US $25,000,000.

You can read more about this subject at the SEC website:

SEC – 17 CFR Parts 275 and 279

[Release No. IA-2333; File No. S7-30-04] RIN 3235-AJ25

Registration Under the Advisers Act of Certain Hedge Fund Advisers

http://sec.gov/rules/final/ia-2333.htm

Consider risks and opportunities before investing in hedge funds. You have to evaluate if they match your risk tolerance. They have a reward potential, but also have risks related to the limited information often provided to investors. Some hedge funds also implement risky strategies.

U.S. domiciled hedge funds are structured as Limited Partnerships. Offshore funds are, usually, structured as corporations and are not limited to a given number of investors. A Limited Partnership is a private investment vehicle that invests in a venture for financial gain. You can enter the partnership through a brokerage firm, or the arrangement can be private.

The partnership provides a General Partner and investors, who are Limited Partners. A Limited Partner is required to be an accredited investor that the SEC defines as an individual who has a net worth of at least $1 million or annual net income of more than $200,000 if single or $300,000 if married. An institution must have a net worth of at least $5 million. The exposure to loss of Limited Partners is limited to their investment.

Most hedge funds are structured as open-end funds. Investors may often redeem shares on a quarterly basis, although some funds require even longer periods. In this way, a fund can optimize the liquidity and its strategy implementation.

Hedge funds charge a management fee based on a percentage of assets under management (1% to 2% on average). There is also typically a performance fee established in proportion to profitability. On average, hedge funds charge between 10% and 20% of gross returns. Sometimes, the performance fees are levied when a performance target is met.

Most hedge funds aim for a risk-adjusted absolute return. As they use a wide range of financial instruments, they can be very flexible.

Following is a list of categories of the main investment styles applied by hedge funds according to the Credit Suisse First Boston Tremont Index (you can read about the Index at:
www.hedgeindex.com/hedgeindex/en/default.aspx?cy=USD):

- **Convertible Arbitrage** consists of hedge investing in convertible securities. A typical approach is to be long the convertible bond and short the stock.

- **Dedicated Short Bias**, with which the fund manager invests mainly in equities and derivatives, maintaining net short exposure

- **Emerging Markets** implements an equity or fixed income strategy. Funds often employ a long-only strategy

- **Equity Market Neutral** seeks to exploit market inefficiencies, usually, being simultaneously long and short within the same sector, industry, capitalization, country, etc

- **Event-Driven** consists of exploiting the price movement generated by a corporate event related to distressed stocks, mergers, takeovers, news, etc. In particular:

  - **Risk Arbitrage** funds manage long and short positions in both companies involved in a merger or acquisition

  - **Distressed Securities** funds invest in debt, equity or trade claims of companies

- **Fixed Income Arbitrage** intends to profit from price anomalies between related interest-rate securities

- **Global Macro** implements long and short positions in major capital or derivative markets, depending on the interpretation of economic trends

- **Long/Short Equity** consists of equity-oriented investing, without being market neutral. These funds can implement various styles, value and growth, and small-cap and large-cap stocks with a net long and short position. Futures and options may be used for hedging. Investments may be related to a country, an industry or a sector

- **Managed Futures** is applied in futures and currency markets. Commodity Trading Advisors (CTAs) apply systematic or discretionary strategies

- **Multi-Strategy** implements an investment approach diversifying by employing various strategies simultaneously to realize short- and long-term gains

You can find general information about hedge funds at: http://en.wikipedia.org/wiki/Hedge_fund.

Additional information about hedge funds can be found at the Hedge Fund Association website (www.thehfa.org/Aboutus.cfm) and the Lipper HedgeWorld website (www.hedgeworld.com).

In particular, HedgeWorld provides access to industry news, research and events. The LipperTASS database provides research on more than 4,000 hedge funds.

A fund of hedge funds is an investment company that invests in hedge funds. Some funds are registered with the SEC under the Investment Company Act of 1940 and must provide investors with a prospectus and the SEC with a quarterly report. Investment minimums can be lower than those of hedge funds.

There are two main categories of fund of hedge funds

- **Diversified funds** – assets are invested in various types of hedge funds.

- **Niche funds** – assets are invested in funds of a similar type/strategy

Some funds of hedge funds may charge another 1% to 3% fee on top of the fees charged by underlying funds.

For additional information about funds of hedge funds, you can read the following document:

SEC

Hedging Your Bets:

A Heads Up on Hedge Funds and Funds of Hedge Funds

www.sec.gov/answers/hedge.htm

Interesting sources of information to understand issues related to hedge funds are the following documents:

Implications of the Growth of Hedge Funds
Staff Report to the

United States Securities and Exchange Commission

September 2003

www.sec.gov/news/studies/hedgefunds0903.pdf

SEC Roundtable on Hedge Funds

May 2003

www.connectlive.com/events/sechedgefunds

Stocks

Stocks represent the ownership of corporate assets, net of corporate liabilities. Their value depends on corporate assets, liabilities and income, and other factors. The perception by traders and investors of how the business will be run in the future is also important.

The two main categories of stocks are common stock and preferred stock. Preferred stockholders normally do not have voting rights. They are entitled to dividends that must be paid out before payment of the dividend on the common stock. They also have a priority when trying to recover their investment should the company fail or liquidate.

Common stock generally entitles the shareholder to one vote for every share owned. Some companies have different classes of common stock. Class A and Class B stocks might provide shareholders with different voting rights, but it can also happen that a given class does not provide voting rights. As an example, Berkshire Hathaway Inc. has two classes of common stock designated Class A and Class B. A share of Class B common stock has the rights of 1/30th of a share of Class A common stock except that a Class B share has 1/200th of the voting rights of a Class A share (rather than 1/30th of the vote). Each share of a Class A common stock is convertible at any time into 30 shares of Class B common stock, but holders of Class B shares are not able to convert them into Class A shares. This mechanism allows arbitrage between the two types of stock.

A dividend is a part of a company's earnings that is returned to shareholders. Companies use dividends to distribute a portion of profits to their shareholders. Companies have no legal obligation to pay dividends, but they will pay them to preferred shareholders unless the company is experiencing financial troubles. Sometimes, companies assign a stock dividend with new shares being distributed to shareholders. An advantage of a stock dividend is that shareholders do not generally have to pay taxes on the value. The dividend payment date, the amount of the dividend and the ex-dividend date are established on the declaration date. On the record date, the company compiles a list of shareholders that will receive the dividend. The payout will be available to those investors who own the stock before the ex-dividend date. The dividend payout automatically reduces the value of the company. The companies that have a policy of distributing dividends often operate in mature sectors. These companies have a stable business and follow a policy of earnings distribution to their shareholders.

When a corporation splits its shares, it distributes additional shares to shareholders. The stock-market capitalization remains the same and there is no effect on the worth of the company. The split may be interpreted by investors as a sign of confidence in the company's future returns. It increases the number of shares on the market and therefore increases liquidity, especially for small trade-sizes.

A buyback is a corporation's repurchase of previously issued stocks, reducing the number of outstanding shares. A buyback is generally considered a sign of optimism about the future of the company. It may indicate also that the management believes the current price is undervalued. The decision to repurchase stocks also helps improve the company's financial ratios, which is actually a questionable motivation. When shareholders authorize a buyback, the company has no obligation to actually undertake it. Buyback plans are a sign of confidence, but it has to be verified that the repurchase is executed as announced.

You can read about buybacks at:
www.investopedia.com/articles/02/041702.asp.

Listed stocks have ticker symbols. Each exchange assigns ticker symbols to its instruments. The one-character symbols are rare, and therefore exchanges usually reserve them for the largest firms. NASDAQ National Market System stocks have four-character ticker symbols. NASDAQ SmallCap stocks have five-character ticker symbols. U.S. open-end mutual funds have five-character ticker symbols, the last character of which is always X.

Note: since the end of January 2007, NASDAQ has been able to display also one-, two- and three-character stock symbols in addition to the traditional four-character symbols. The SEC has requested the exchanges to develop a Symbology Plan for selecting and allocating securities symbols across exchanges.

There is also another way of uniquely identifying not only stocks, but financial instruments in general, including government and municipal bonds. It represents a uniform security identification system and it is the CUSIP (Committee on Uniform Securities Identifying Procedures) number.

The CUSIP Service Bureau, operated by Standard & Poor's for the American Bankers Association, has the purpose of identifying issuers and issues of financial instruments within a standard framework, and disseminating these data. CUSIP numbers and descriptions are used in the financial industry and are important for the process of clearance and settlement of securities.

The CUSIP number consists of nine characters: a base number of six characters known as the issuer number and a two character suffix known as the issue number. The ninth character is a check digit.

For more details see: www.investopedia.com/ask/answers/04/040704.asp

and the CUSIP Service Bureau website: www.cusip.com/static/html/cusipaccess/whats.html#send

Find the CUSIP numbers for the various securities at the Fidelity Investments site:

http://activequote.fidelity.com/mmnet/SymLookup.phtml?QUOTE_TYPE=&scCode=E&searchBy=S&searchFor=wmt&submit=Search

There are different ways to categorize stocks:

- **Blue-Chips** are solid and reliable companies with a history of growth and stability.

- **Growth stocks** refer to companies experiencing a fast growth rate. These companies have a low payout of their earnings because they need to finance expansion. They are characterized by high volatility, but also high reward potential

- **Value stocks** present a low price relative to the fundamentals. They tend to be mature companies in older industries. They have a high dividend yield, low price-to-book ratio and/or low price-to-earnings ratio

- **Cyclical stocks** are related to companies whose earnings are significantly influenced by macroeconomic trends. These companies suffer during recessions and do well during economic expansions. Examples include stocks of industrial sectors (automobile, steel, etc.) and housing

- **Defensive stocks** are issued related to companies less sensitive to the economic cycle, such as food, beverages, drugs and insurance

You can also refer to stocks by their size, according to the market capitalization of a company. The definitions might vary, but usually they are as follows:

- **Large-cap** have a market value of more than $10 billion.

- **Mid-cap** have a market value between $2 billion and $10 billion.

- **Small-cap** have a market value between $300 million and $2 billion.

In general, the larger the cap size, the lower the volatility of the stock. Small-cap and mid-cap companies usually have a higher potential for future growth than large-cap companies, but their stock has a higher volatility.

Stocks can also be organized into sectors. Utilities and consumer staples are said to be defensive sectors. Transportation, technology, healthcare, financial, energy, consumer cyclical, basic materials, capital goods, and communications services are considered cyclical.

A penny stock is characterized by low price (usually between \$1 and \$5) and low market capitalization. Typically, penny stocks are those of small companies with illiquid and speculative shares. They should be considered high-risk investments. These companies are often subject to limited listing requirements with fewer filing and regulatory standards. They often trade over the counter through the OTCBB and the Pink Sheets. There have been many cases of fraud involving these stocks. Spamming on the internet on these stocks is frequent.

A tracking stock is issued by a parent company and tracks the performance of a specific subsidiary or line of business of the company. It is also a security specifically designed to mirror the performance of an index. The most popular tracking stock is the QQQQ, which mirrors the returns of the NASDAQ 100 index. To read about QQQQ, see:

www.nasdaq.com/indexshares/nasdaq100.stm.

A useful indicator of risk is beta, which measures the systematic risk, or volatility, indicating the degree to which the price of a security moves compared with the market as a whole. It provides a sense of the stock's risk compared with the market. It is used also to compare risk of different stocks. A beta of 1 indicates that the security's price tends to move with the market. A beta greater than 1 indicates that the security's price tends to be more volatile than the market, and a beta less than 1 means it tends to be less volatile than the market. Utility stocks tend to have a low beta and, conversely, high-tech stocks have a high beta. Beta is based on historical data, which does not predict future beta or future volatility.

To learn the basics of beta see:

www.investopedia.com/articles/01/102401.asp

www.investopedia.com/articles/stocks/04/113004.asp

http://en.wikipedia.org/wiki/Beta_coefficient

ETFs – Exchange-Traded Funds

Exchange-traded funds are an instrument also popular among individual investors. The investment objective is to achieve the same return as a particular market index. ETFs are baskets of securities traded on an exchange. The most important stock indexes, such as the Dow Jones Industrial Average (DJIA), Standard & Poor's 500, and the NASDAQ Composite, have ETFs based on them. There are ETFs for stock sectors, real-estate investment trusts, international stock indexes, bonds, and so forth. They are passively managed, tracking a variety of sector-specific, country-specific, and broad-market indexes. ETFs are legally classified as open-end companies or Unit Investment Trusts (UITs). Investors buy creation units and shares can be sold to other investors on the secondary market, or they can sell the creation units back to the ETF.

Through ETFs, the average investor can focus on different asset classes, allowing diversification at low cost. Small investors are able to build and implement their own asset allocation and market strategy.

You can invest in many different sectors and markets by buying an index and following the index fluctuations passively. Actively managed funds have higher commissions and, often, they perform worse than the benchmark due to management costs and the marketing structure.

Unlike most mutual funds, ETFs can be bought and sold at any time during the day, the same way you trade a stock. They can be sold short and bought on margin. Many ETFs are currently traded at the AMEX. ETF expenses are normally lower than the least-costly index mutual funds. You pay a commission to buy and sell ETF shares, plus low annual operating expenses, which are paid proportionally to the time you are invested in the ETF. They do not trade at the net asset values of their holdings. The price is determined by forces of supply and demand on the market. In fact, ETFs can trade at prices above or below the value of their portfolio of securities. Discounts or premiums are usually low. Arbitrage opportunities ensure that prices close the gap between the ETF's market price and its net asset value.

Index ETFs: These are passive index funds. They allow investors to trade a portfolio of securities in a single transaction. These funds allow investors to trade on indexes such as the S&P, Russell, and Dow Jones, but also international indexes. An index ETF can represent a specific sector or industry or a specific basket of stocks. Funds may focus on specific investment styles such as value or growth.

The AMEX has been the first exchange to list index ETFs. The NYSE and the CBOE have added these types of funds to their range of products, trying to leverage on their growth.

Closed-End ETF: Capital raised through an IPO is invested according to the ETF objectives. Traditional open-end mutual funds issue and redeem shares of investors at net asset value. When an investor purchases or sells shares of a closed-end ETF, it is done on a national exchange such as the NYSE or AMEX. Different from an open-end fund, the shares of a closed-end ETF remain constant. However, additional shares can be created through secondary offerings, dividend reinvestment, or rights offerings.

Examples of ETF classification are:

- Sector

- Regional

- Global

- Large-Cap

- Total Market

- Country

- Bonds

- Mid-Cap

- Small-Cap

- Growth

- Value

Popular ETFs are:

ETF	Ticker	Exchange	Remarks
Standard & Poor's 500 Index Depository Receipts	SPY	AMEX	Spiders tracks the S&P 500.
NASDAQ-100 Index Tracking Stock	QQQ	AMEX	It tracks the NASDAQ-100 index, which includes 100 of the largest companies listed on the NASDAQ stock market based on market capitalization.
DIAMONDS Trust	DIA	AMEX	DIA tracks the DJIA, composed of 30 blue-chip stocks.
iShares S & P 500	IVV	AMEX	As SPY, this Barclay's ETF tracks the S&P 500.
Standard & Poor's MidCap 400 SPDRs	MDY	AMEX	It tracks the S&P MidCap 400 index, which measures the performance of mid-size U.S. companies.
iShares Russell 2000	IWM	AMEX	It tracks the Russell 2000 index, a benchmark for mid- and small-cap companies.
iShares MSCI Japan	EWJ	AMEX	EWJ is designed to track the price of securities in the Japanese market, measured by the MSCI Japan Index.
Total Stock Market VIPERs	VTI	AMEX	The Vanguard Group's VTI tracks the Wilshire 5000 broad market index.
iShares SmallCap 600	IJR	AMEX	This ETF tracks the S&P SmallCap 600, which measures the performance of the small-cap US companies.
Energy Select Sector SPDR	XLE	AMEX	The Energy Select Sector SPDR Fund is an exchange-traded fund designed to replicate the price performance of the Energy Sector Index. There are nine Select Sector SPDR Funds. To learn more about SPDRs visit: www.sectorspdr.com.

An ETF, like any other type of investment company, has to provide a prospectus to investors. Some ETFs also deliver a prospectus to secondary market purchasers. As an alternative, they can give investors a Product Description, which summarizes key information about the ETF.

Before purchasing ETF shares, you should carefully read all of an ETF's available information, including its prospectus.

For more information about ETFs see:

www.sec.gov/answers/etf.htm

www.sec.gov/answers/mfinfo.htm

Interesting websites where you can find information on available ETFs are:

www.etfconnect.com

http://etf.stock-encyclopedia.com

www.interactivebrokers.co.uk/contract_info

DRs – Depositary Receipts

Depositary Receipts (DRs) were created in 1927 to aid U.S. investors, who wished to purchase shares of foreign corporations. Each DR denotes Depositary Shares (DSs) representing a specific number of underlying shares on deposit with a custodian in the issuer's home market.

DRs are denominated in U.S. dollars and are subject to the trading and settlement procedures of the market in which they trade. DRs allow traders to avoid international settlement and facilitate diversification into non-U.S. securities.

The American Depositary Receipt (ADR) is a negotiable instrument issued by a U.S. depositary bank, representing one or more shares or a fraction of a share of a non-U.S. company. Individual shares of a foreign corporation represented by an ADR are called American Depositary Shares (ADSs).

The concept of the ADR has been extended to other markets, resulting in instruments known as Global Depositary Receipts (GDRs), International Depositary Receipts (IDRs), and European Depositary Receipts (EDRs), which are generally traded or listed in two or more international markets outside the issuer's home country.

Although ADRs are U.S. dollar denominated securities and pay dividends in U.S. dollars, they do not eliminate the currency risk associated with an investment in a non-U.S. company.

Banks purchase shares from the company, bundle the shares into groups, and reissue the ADRs. DRs are listed on either the NYSE, AMEX or NASDAQ or in the OTC market (through the OTCBB and/or the Pink Sheets). DRs are bought and sold just like any other stock. The depositary bank sets the ratio of DRs per home-country share. DRs can be issued as a public offering of securities on a U.S. exchange or privately placed.

There are three different types of DR issues:

- **Level 1** – DRs trade in the U.S. in the OTC market. Information can be accessed through the Pink Sheets and/or the OTCBB. Through this program the issuer aims to enlarge its U.S. investor base. Normally target investors are larger institutions who enable execute trades with securities not listed on an exchange. They have minimum requirements from the SEC.

- **Level 2** – This type of DR is listed on an exchange (NYSE, AMEX, NASDAQ). Together with level 3, it requires full registration with the SEC.

- **Level 3** – The issuer offers new shares to U.S. investors in the form of DRs. A public offering allows the issuer to raise capital accessing the US investor base. This program provides the issuer's with visibility within the U.S.

Other instruments are also aimed to access additional markets and investors. They are the American Depositary Debentures (ADDs) and American Depositary Notes (ADNs). ADDs and ADNs are debt securities issued in the U.S. that represent, respectively, debentures or notes of the issuer deposited with the depositary's custodian in the issuer's home market.

To find informative content about Depositary Receipts, you can read the Citibank DR Information Guide at: http://wwss.citissb.com/adr/www.

An important role is played by The Depository Trust & Clearing Corporation (DTCC) (www.dtcc.com), which provides "clearance, settlement and information services for equities, corporate and municipal bonds, government and mortgage-backed securities and Over-the-Counter credit derivatives".

DTCC's depository (DTC) provides custody and services for more than 2 million securities issues from the U.S. and 100 other countries and territories.

DTC works with depositaries to facilitate the issuance and cancellation of DRs, to transfer and deliver DRs to the broker, to manage dividends distribution, and other activities such as custody, settlement, etc.

For more information see American Depositary Receipts:

www.sec.gov/answers/adrs.htm

http://en.wikipedia.org/wiki/American_Depositary_Receipt#Level_I

www.investopedia.com/university/adr/

International Investing:

www.sec.gov/investor/pubs/ininvest.htm

IPOs – Initial Public Offerings

Issues trade in primary markets when issuers first create and sell them. Primary trading in new equity issues takes place in the Initial Public Offering market. Trading then occurs in secondary markets.

Issuers may use underwriters to support them when selling their securities. In best-efforts offering, the underwriter acts strictly as a broker. In an underwriting offering, the underwriter guarantees the issuer an offering price. If the underwriter cannot sell the securities at the offering price, the underwriter buys them for its own account. In a fixed-price offering, the underwriter establishes a price and buyers subscribe to the offering. If the offering is oversubscribed, the underwriter allocates the shares.

When a private corporation intends to raise additional capital, it can either take on debt or sell partial ownership. In an IPO, the corporation chooses to sell ownership to the public. Corporations go public mainly because capital raised through an IPO does not have to be repaid, while debt securities must be repaid with interest. The drawback to an IPO is that owners of the corporation lose part of their ownership.

The IPO process starts when the corporation files a registration statement, according to the Securities Act of 1933, with the SEC. The SEC then investigates the registration statement and approves the full disclosure. The underwriter first issues a preliminary prospectus and then an official prospectus before or along with the stock offering. After the SEC approval, the price and date of the IPO are decided.

Especially during speculative bubbles, there may be a big difference between the price of the IPO and the secondary market trading due to the excess of demand for the securities object of the IPO with respect to the supply. In these conditions, it is difficult for the individual investor to have the shares assigned during the IPO.

For more information see:

www.sec.gov/answers/ipo.htm

www.sec.gov/answers/ipodiff.htm

IPOs may be the target of speculation and be characterized by a highly volatile environment. Beginners should be prudent when deciding to enter new positions in this type of market. What could happen is that investors who did not have the shares assigned during the IPO might buy them at much higher prices during the secondary market trading. After an initial spike, prices would then fall. As a general consideration, it is often difficult to evaluate the value of companies without a proven track record and all the necessary information.

Investing in an IPO is a risky and speculative investment. Only active traders, depending on their investment objectives and risk tolerance, should consider this type of investment.

In a Direct Public Offering (DPO) shares are purchased directly from the issuing company. DPOs give the average investor a chance to invest in a public offering. A company can raise capital by its own customers, employees, and so forth. DPOs do not occur frequently and are less expensive for companies than IPOs.

For more information about this subject see:

Speech by SEC Acting chair: *Raising Capital on the Internet*

Remarks by Acting Chair Laura S. Unger

At the 2001 Corporate Law Symposium

University of Cincinnati School of Law

March 9, 2001

www.sec.gov/news/speech/spch471.htm

General information about IPOs can be found at:

www.investopedia.com/university/ipo

http://en.wikipedia.org/wiki/Initial_public_offering

Futures

In the 19th century, farmers and merchants began using forward agreements called "to arrive" contracts, which allowed them to lock in the price and deliver the grain later at a specified date. These contracts were useful for hedging and speculating, but they could not eliminate the risk of default among the parties involved.

Exchanges, then, started to require a deposit with a third party as a "guarantee." These contracts were standardized around 1865 and in 1925 the first futures clearing house was formed. A standardized contract specified quality and unit of measurement for each commodity traded.

Futures contracts are traded on organized exchanges in a variety of instruments. In the 70's, most futures trading was in agricultural commodities, such as corn and wheat. Today, futures markets offer trading also in non-agricultural commodities, including metals such as gold, silver, and copper, and fuels such as crude oil and natural gas. The most widely traded futures contracts, however, are in financial instruments, such as interest rates, foreign currencies, and stock indexes. Single-stock futures began trading only in November 2002. Open outcry has been the principal environment to trade futures contracts for a long time. The trading pit is still popular in agricultural and other commodity markets. During the past few years, however, electronic trading has become a competitive challenge from the cost and speed-of-execution perspective.

Futures contracts are standardized to include the contract size, the delivery months, the last trading day, and the delivery period and location. Additionally, elements of standardization are also related to the tick size, the daily price limit, the quality specifications and the contract trading hours.

Standardization enhances liquidity, as it is possible for market participants to trade the same instrument, and the use of futures instruments for hedging. Nowadays, most futures contracts do not result in physical delivery.

Futures trades are cleared through a clearing organization. A clearing house acts as a third party to futures and options contracts, in particular as a buyer to every clearing member seller, and as a seller to every buyer. When you execute a transaction, you are technically buying or selling, having the clearing organization as your counterpart.

Members clear their trades through the clearing house at the end of each session. Clearing organizations provide clearing, netting, and settlement services for futures and other derivatives for its members. They ensure the conduct of delivery procedures, and collect and maintain margin monies. A clearing organization may be a division of an exchange, but also a separate entity.

You can find a list of registered clearing organizations at the Commodity Futures Trading Commission (CFTC) website:

Derivatives Clearing Organizations (DCOs)
http://services.cftc.gov/SIRT/SIRT.aspx?Topic=ClearingOrganizations&impl icit=true&type=DCO&CustomColumnDisplay=TTTTTTTT

The CFTC is an independent agency, which has the mandate "to regulate commodity futures and option markets in the U.S." The mandate has been renewed recently by the Commodity Futures Modernization Act of 2000 (CFMA).

"The mission of the Commodity Futures Trading Commission (CFTC) is to protect market users and the public from fraud, manipulation, and abusive practices related to the sale of commodity and financial futures and options, and to foster open, competitive, and financially sound futures and option markets." (www.cftc.gov/cftc/cftchome.htm)

The standardization of futures contracts allows buyers and sellers to liquidate a purchase or a short sale through the sale or the purchase of an equal number of contracts of the same delivery month. They "offset" their obligation to take delivery on the underlying instrument or commodity of the futures contract. The offset consists of taking a second futures or options position opposite to the initial position.

As an example, if a trader buys one December CME E-mini S&P contract, he must sell one December CME E-mini S&P contract before the contract calls for delivery. Since you technically buy from and sell your futures contract to the same party, the clearing house, you offset your position and the contract is extinguished. This process is quite different from the forward market where, when you buy a contract and then sell an identical one to a different party, you have obligations under two separate contracts.

A cash-settlement process (for example on stock index futures) allows, upon expiry or exercise, the seller of the instrument to transfer only the associated cash position without physical delivery. In some cases, a trader has to be ready and accept the delivery of the underlying commodity. Futures contracts for most physical commodities require the delivery. The responsibility of delivery makes futures prices follow the cash value of the underlying asset.

Both buyers and sellers are required to post a margin (or performance bond) determined by the exchange or clearing organization generally of an amount about 2-10% of the contract value. It is called "initial margin" (or initial performance bond) and it represents a deposit paid as a guarantee to indicate that the traders will be able to fulfil the contract. The margin requirement is a function of the price volatility of the instrument. Firms must request of their clients at least the minimum amounts set by the exchange, but they are also allowed to establish higher margins.

At the end of each session, a trader's position is "marked-to-the-market" and the account is settled on a cash basis. Very simply, money is added to the account balance if the position displays a profit for that day. On the contrary, money is deducted from the account if the position has printed a loss. The account is rebalanced every day after the close of the trading session.

When the amount of money in an account drops below the "maintenance margin" level (performance bond) because of daily losses, a trader is asked to increase funds to bring the account up to the initial level. Margin calls can be issued at any time if the market price fluctuation necessitates the addition of funds to return above the specified level.

The following are margins required to trade some E-mini contracts. Margin rates change daily and this information is reported only to provide a rough idea of the amount of money required to open a position.

Description	Initial margin	Maint margin
E-MINI RUSSELL	$4,000	$3,200
E-MINI S&P INDX	$3,500	$2,800
MINI 5X DOW FUT	$2,813	$2,250
MINI CRUDE NYM	$2,363	$1,750
MINI EURO IMM	$1,148	$850
MINI EURODLR	$338	$250
MINI #2 HT OIL NYM	$2,869	$2,125
E-MINI MIDCAP 400	$3,750	$3,000
MINI NASDAQ INDX	$3,250	$2,600
MINI NAT GAS NY	$1,688	$1,250
MINI GOLD	$905	$670
MINI SILVER	$945	$700
MINI NY UNL GAS	$3,206	$2,375
MINI YEN IMM	$1,080	$800

Futures are assigned a one- or two-character code (the ticker symbol) that identifies the contract type. In addition to that, you have to also know the month and year code. For instance, if you were trading the E-mini December S&P future in 2007, the code would be ESZ07.

Month Codes	
• January	F
• February	G
• March	H
• April	J
• May	K
• June	M
• July	N
• August	Q
• September	U
• October	V
• November	X
• December	Z

You can obtain a full list of contract symbols at the various exchanges websites.

Each futures contract has a minimum price increment called tick. The value of a trading session's move can be calculated as in the following example. If the E-mini S&P future moves up 40 ticks in one day (10 points) , the value of the contract will increase $500 (40 ticks x $12.50 tick value = $500).

The CME E-mini S&P 500 multiplier is $50, which means that 1 point change in the contract value is worth $50. If the S&P 500 futures index level is 1400, it means that the instrument value is 1400 x $50 = $70,000 per contract.

The open interest of a contract indicates the number of futures positions that are not closed at the end of the trading session. Open interest has three components: large traders, small traders and commercials. Futures positions are classified as commercial if a trader uses futures contracts in that particular instrument for hedging. Some analysts assume that open interest and prices should move in the same direction to confirm the ongoing trend. Divergences may be the sign of a trend reversal. The strength of a trend can be assessed through the analysis of volume. In this regard, low volume levels and high open interest may indicate that commercial participation is high. High volume and low open interest may indicate that speculation is active, with day traders as the main players who close their position at the end of the session.

Traders willing to use these concepts operatively, however, should get into the details quantifying the assessments. Finally, on many instruments there is a great deal of arbitrage going on (for example in the E-minis), which needs to be taken into account as it is not supply/demand volume.

The Commitments of Traders (COT) report, published by the CFTC provides a breakdown of each Tuesday's open interest for markets. The weekly reports for Futures-Only Commitments of Traders and for Futures-and-Options-Combined Commitments of Traders are released every Friday.

Reports are available in both a short and long format. The reports show open interest, spreading, changes from the previous report, percentages of open interest by category, and numbers of traders.

Below you can see an example of a report related to the E-mini S&P futures contract:

E-MINI S&P 500 STOCK INDEX – CHICAGO MERCANTILE EXCHANGE

FUTURES ONLY POSITIONS AS OF 12/26/06|

NON-COMMERCIAL			COMMERCIAL		TOTAL		NONREPORTABLE POSITIONS	
LONG	SHORT	SPREADS	LONG	SHORT	LONG	SHORT	LONG	SHORT

OPEN INTEREST: 1,489,606

COMMITMENTS

LONG	SHORT	SPREADS	LONG	SHORT	LONG	SHORT	LONG	SHORT
298,877	216,573	26,942	861,400	1,134,015	1,187,219	1,377,530	3,02,387	1,12,076

CHANGES FROM 12/19/06 (CHANGE IN OPEN INTEREST:-15,330)

LONG	SHORT	SPREADS	LONG	SHORT	LONG	SHORT	LONG	SHORT
-49,876	-21,378	-962	17,499	20,764	-33,339	-1,576	18,009	-13,754

PERCENT OF OPEN INTEREST FOR EACH CATEGORY OF TRADERS

LONG	SHORT	SPREADS	LONG	SHORT	LONG	SHORT	LONG	SHORT
20.1	14.5	1.8	57.8	76.1	79.7	92.5	20.3	7.5

NUMBER OF TRADERS IN EACH CATEGORY (TOTAL TRADERS: 242)

73	56	26	72	66	56	137

When deciding the type of futures contract to trade, you should consider a number of factors. Wide daily ranges and volatility present good profit opportunities for day traders, but also increased risk. In this market, commissions impact less on your results. A liquid market presents a very limited bid/ask spread. A small contract size reduces the amount of money you put at risk, which is important for small trading accounts. Margin requirements too close to the size of your trading account may cause a margin call.

You can check online the background of firms and individuals involved in the futures industry by using NFA's Background Affiliation Status Information Center (BASIC). NFA, the CFTC and the U.S. futures exchanges have supplied the database with relevant information (www.nfa.futures.org/basicnet).

For education and publications about futures see:

www.nfa.futures.org/investor/investorLearningCenter.asp

www.cftc.gov/cftc/cftcreports.htm#Brochures

www.cftc.gov/educationcenter/index.htm

A lot of valuable information can be also found at the exchanges' websites.

References:

www.futuresindustry.org

www.nfa.futures.org

www.cftc.gov

Options

Options on futures contracts are a relatively recent instrument as they were introduced only in 1982. Offered initially as part of a pilot program, their success eventually brought a wide range of options available today on the market on agricultural and financial futures contracts. An option is a contract that provides the right, but not the obligation, to buy or sell the underlying instrument at a fixed price on or before a specified date. The underlying instrument can be a listed stock, an exchange index, a futures contract, or other. As option contracts depend on underlying instrument values, they are considered derivative contracts.

The writer of an option is the trader who sells the option. The contract is characterized by a strike price, at which the contract may be exercised, and an expiration date, which is the last day on which an option can be either exercised, offset or closed out.

There are three styles of options, which refer to when the option is exercisable. American-style options may be exercised at any time before expiration. European-style options may be exercised only during a specified period, to date on expiration. A capped option will be automatically exercised before expiration when the underlying instrument "hits the cap" for the option.

When you buy an option, you can decide to:

- Exercise the option and take the underlying instrument position at the fixed price

- Liquidate the option and receive the current market value of the premium

- Let the option expire and lose the premium. When it expires, an option has no value and does not exist any more

Each situation depends on the relationship between the current price and the strike price of the option.

There are two types of options: calls and puts. A call is an option to buy the underlying instrument at a fixed strike price at any time during the life of the option. A put option provides the right to sell the underlying instrument at a fixed strike price at any time during the life of the option. You can either be a buyer or a seller of both types of options.

The strike price is the price at which the buyer of a call has the right to purchase the underlying instrument or at which the buyer of a put has the right to sell it. The premium is the cost of an option. It is the amount of money that an option holder (either call or put) is willing to pay and an option writer receives for the rights conveyed by the option. The option buyer's risk is limited to the amount of the premium and the option seller's risk is potentially unlimited.

Options are available for several expiration dates. For example, the buyer of a MAR07 CME E-mini S&P 500 Options call has the right to buy the underlying futures contract at 1440 anytime on or before the option's expiration date. The holder of a MAR07 CME E-mini S&P 500 Options put has the right to sell the underlying futures contract at 1440 on or before the expiration. The premium depends on the futures contract price and the time remaining before expiration.

Options contracts are available at different strike prices. A call option with a strike close to the current futures price has a higher premium than one with a higher strike price. The same concept applies to put options.

An option's premium takes into account intrinsic value and time value. Intrinsic value is the absolute value of the difference between the instrument's price and the option's strike price. Time value represents the portion of the premium, in addition to the intrinsic value, attributable to the time remaining until the option expires and volatility.

For example, consider a CME E-mini S&P 500 futures contract trading at 1380. A call option at a strike price of 1370 would have an intrinsic value of $500. This option is called "in-the-money", as the futures contract price is above the option strike price. A call option "out-of-the-money" has the strike price above the current market price of the underlying instrument. It has no intrinsic value and the premium consists only of time value. A call option "at the money" has the strike price equal to the underlying instrument's market price.

Time decay will accelerate and the option's value will depreciate faster when the option approaches expiration. The rate at which options values change in response to a change in the underlying instrument is called delta. They are near zero for out-of-the-money options and near one for deep in-the-money options.

- **Theta** provides a measure of the rate of change in the value of an option due to the passage of time.

- **Gamma** represents the rate of change between an option delta and the underlying instrument's price.

- **Vega** represents the rate of change between an option value and the underlying instrument's volatility.

When you trade options, you have to be aware of the concept of leverage. Leverage magnifies both gains and losses. As the premium is a limited portion of the underlying assets' value, a small change in the underlying instrument price is reflected in a much larger percentage change (profit or loss) in relation to the premium.

There are options available to implement longer-term strategies up to one or more years. These are called LEAPS (Long Term Equity Anticipation Securities). LEAPS are options with expiration dates of up to three years from the date they are first listed, and are available on a number of individual stocks and indexes. LEAPS are available on widely held issues.

You can apply many different strategies combining the purchase and sale of calls and puts. These strategies can be very complex. For example, you can build a spread trading strategy, which consists of being long one call option with a low strike price and short one call option with a higher strike price. This strategy can be used when you are relatively bullish on market price and/or volatility.

A butterfly spread consists of being short two at-the-money call options, long one in-the-money call option and long one out-of-the-money call option. This strategy can be used when you are neutral on market direction and bearish on volatility. The long butterfly strategy would lead to a profit if the price of the underlying asset remains close to the strike price at which the two calls were sold.

To build a long "straddle", you must buy one call option and buy one put option at the same strike price. This strategy can be used when you are bullish on volatility but are unsure of market direction.

In a long "strangle", you buy one call option with a lower strike price and buy one put option at a higher strike price. This strategy is similar to the straddle.

Each of these strategies profits from different market conditions. Traders have to be quite expert before trading these strategies. The advice is that you study in detail the characteristics of the various strategies. For more information, see: www.888optionsnet.com/select/login.asp?req=DOC-equity_options_strategy_guide.

You can visit the CBOE website for additional information at *Options Concepts*: www.cboe.com/LearnCenter/Concepts/default.aspx.

A valuable tool is the CBOE Options Toolbox, which is an interactive educational program about exchange-traded equity options, index options and LEAPS. It also comprises an options calculator.

The following website explains how to build the different strategies: www.optiontradingtips.com/strategies/index.html.

The CBOE also provides an option price calculator based on Java at: www.cboe.com/LearnCenter/OptionCalculator.aspx.

"The Options Clearing Corporation (OCC) is an equity derivatives clearing organization, which operates under the jurisdiction of both the SEC and the CFTC. OCC clears transactions for put and call options on stocks, stock indexes, foreign currencies, interest rate composites and single-stock futures.

OCC also offers clearing and settlement services for transactions in futures and options on futures." (www.optionsclearing.com/learning_center/opt_ed/get_started.jsp)

The Options Industry Council (OIC) was created in 1992 to educate investors and advisors on equity options. OIC sponsors include the AMEX, the Boston Options Exchange, the CBOE, the International Securities Exchange, NYSE Arca, the PHLX and the OCC.

As a reference, see the documentation available at the OIC website: www.888options.com, including the brochure *Characteristics and risks of standardized options* and others at:

www.optionsclearing.com/publications/risks/riskstoc.pdf

www.optionseducation.org/resources/brochures.jsp

Single stock futures

The current legislation authorizes security futures trading on both futures exchanges and securities exchanges. In the U.S., under the Shad-Johnson Accord, trading in futures on individual equities was prohibited in 1982. It was only on December 21, 2000, that the Commodity Futures Modernization Act of 2000 (the CFMA) was signed.

You can read the Act at:

Commodity Futures Modernization Act of 2000

http://thomas.loc.gov/cgi-bin/query/z?c106:H.R.5660

The CFMA repealed the Shad-Johnson Accord and it permitted trading of futures on narrow-based indexes and single stocks. The Act allows trading of futures contracts based on single stocks and narrow-based stock indexes, with oversight being shared by the Commodity Futures Trading Commission (CFTC) and the SEC. Futures on broad-based security indexes are subject to the exclusive jurisdiction of the CFTC. Futures on narrow-based securities indexes relating to one industry or economic sector are considered security futures products and subject to joint CFTC and SEC jurisdiction.

Narrow-based stock indexes generally consist of a relatively small number of stocks within the same industry or meeting certain other criteria. These futures contracts are traded in the same way and may be settled in cash as broader based stock indexes. The CFMA directed that single stock futures and narrow-based stock indexes be treated as both securities and futures.

Both the SEC and the CFTC exercise broad regulatory authority, including oversight of the regulatory responsibilities of the futures and securities exchanges. A jurisdiction-sharing plan was agreed between the two agencies and the single stock futures (SSF) began trading in November 2002.

To understand the background of the CFMA Act 2000 see:

Testimony Concerning

H.R. 4541, The Commodity Futures Modernization Act of 2000

By Annette L. Nazareth

Director, Division Of Market Regulation

U.S. Securities & Exchange Commission

Before the Committee on Banking and Financial Services

United States House of Representatives

July 19, 2000

www.sec.gov/news/testimony/ts132000.htm

Security futures is the term used to collectively describe futures on individual stocks, narrow-based indexes and ETFs. SSFs are contracts between two parties to purchase or sell at a specified date a determined quantity of shares of a single equity security at a certain price. The contract is completed at expiration or, in most cases, by offset prior to the expiration date. SSFs are exchange-traded contracts based on an underlying stock. They are very similar to existing futures contracts for grains, metals, bonds, stock indexes and so forth.

A futures contract related to a security does not provide share rights or dividends. These contracts are standardized and specify:

- Contract Size – 100 shares of underlying security.

- Contract Expiration – up to three quarterly and two serial months for a total of four expirations per product class for most single stock and ETF futures. Generally the cycle provides March (H), June (M), September (U) and December (Z). Expiries for the longest term contracts range from six to eight months.

- Minimum Price Fluctuation (Tick Size) – $0.01 x 100 shares = $1.00

- Last Trading Day – third Friday of the expiration month

- Settlement / Delivery – Physical delivery of underlying security on third business day following the expiration day

- Contracts will be cleared through the OCC or the CME (Chicago Mercantile Exchange) clearing house

Initially, SSFs began trading in two U.S. markets: OneChicago and the NQLX. The NQLX was formed as a partnership between the NASDAQ Stock Market and the LIFFE. In June 2003, NASDAQ sold its ownership in the joint venture entirely to Euronext.

NQLX suspended trading in all of its securities futures products in December 2004.

At OneChicago, futures on single stocks and ETFs are physically delivered at expiration date. Futures on narrow-based indexes are cash settled.

The margin, generally, is 20% of the cash value of contract, but the requirement may be lower when the investor holds offsetting positions in the same securities account.

Find contract specifications and listings at:

www.onechicago.com/030000_products/oc_030000.html

Buyers' and sellers' gains/losses are credited/debited daily to traders' accounts, based on the close of the trading session.

Security futures can be used to manage and limit price risks, as a hedging instrument in alternative to options. Traders may also use SSFs to speculate on a stock's performance relative to another stock or hedge holdings against the risk of an adverse price change.

SSFs allow you to modify a portfolio's composition without purchasing or liquidating stocks. Foreign investors can reduce currency risk. It is cheap to leverage a long stock position or to initiate a short position. SSFs are also an opportunity for improved cash flow.

You can find more information about single stock futures at:
www.investopedia.com/articles/optioninvestor/06/SingleStockFutures.asp

http://onechicago.com/010000_learningctr/images/OC_Non_Prof_Bro_5.pdf

An interesting article about futures and associated risks can be found at the NASD website:

Security Futures - Know Your Risks, or Risk Your Future

http://www.finra.org/InvestorInformation/InvestmentChoices/NewFinancial Products/index.htm

Fixed-income securities

Bonds are debt securities issued by corporations and governments that borrow funds from investors for a defined period of time at a specified interest rate.

A bond's value depends on interest rates, rating of the issuer and assets pledged. Bond prices are quoted as a percentage of their par value, which is 100. Some debt issues may be redeemed by the issuer prior to the maturity date. Many instruments are issued in multiples of $1,000 face amounts.

Fixed income can be divided into different asset classes.

A **government bond** is issued by a national government. This includes Treasury bills, Treasury notes, and Treasury bonds. Bonds issued in foreign currencies are referred to as sovereign bonds. Bills mature in one year or less and they do not pay interest, but they sell at a discount of their face value. Notes have a maturity varying from two to five years. Bonds normally mature 10 or more years after they are issued.

To learn more about U.S. Treasury marketable securities, you can explore: www.treasurydirect.gov/RT/RTGateway?page=institHome.

Municipal bonds are issued by a state, city, other local government, or their agencies. The interest income is exempt from federal income tax, and often state and local income taxes as well. General obligation bonds are issued to raise capital to cover expenses and are supported by the taxing power of the issuer. Revenue bonds are issued to fund infrastructure projects and are backed by the income of the projects. You can read the basics of municipal bonds at:

www.investopedia.com/articles/bonds/05/022805.asp

www.investinginbonds.com/learnmore.asp?catid=5&subcatid=24

www.msrb.org/msrb1

A **Corporate bond** is issued by a corporation. Compared with government bonds, they have a higher risk of default. Most corporate bonds are not secured by physical asset or collateral (they are debentures). Investors assume interest rate risk and credit risk.

You can find information about corporate bonds at the SEC site: www.sec.gov/answers/bondcrp.htm.

Credit ratings are published by agencies such as Moody's, Standard and Poor's and Fitch IBCA to categorize credit risk. Ratings range between highest credit quality and default. Long-term credit ratings are indicated with a letter. A triple A (AAA) is the highest credit quality, and C or D (depending on the agency) is the lowest quality. There are different degrees for each rating, which, depending on the agency, have different meaning.

Generally speaking, you can distinguish between investment grade bonds and "junk" bonds, which present a high credit risk. The term "junk" is reserved for bonds with Standard & Poor's ratings below BBB and/or Moody's ratings below Baa.

You can read about the Standard & Poor's Long-term Issue Credit Ratings at:

www2.standardandpoors.com/portal/site/sp/en/us/page.article/2,1,1,4,11484 51187257.html#ID211

Moody's ratings definitions can be found at:

www.moodysasia.com/SHPTContent.ashx?source=StaticContent/Free%20P ages/MDCS/Asia/Rating%20Symbols%20and%20Definitions.pdf

www.moodys.com/moodys/sbin/login/LoginPg.aspx?reqURL=%2Fcust%2F loadbusline%2Easp%3Fbusline%3Dcredit%2Bpolicy

Fitch definitions can be found at:

www.fitchibca.com/corporate/fitchResources.cfm?detail=1

Straight bonds pay interest periodically until maturity. Investors assume that interest payments of investment grade bonds will be made on time. Speculative grade bonds provide higher yields to compensate the risk that the issuers will default payments. Zero coupons pay no interest. They return their principal value at maturity and buyers will buy them at a discount from their face value. A convertible bond provides the holder with the faculty to exchange the bond for stock under certain conditions. These bonds combine the characteristics of a straight bond and an option.

Read www.investinginbonds.com/learnmore.asp?catid=5&subcatid=18 for detailed information about corporate bonds.

Treasury Inflation-Protected Securities (TIPS) are bonds indexed to inflation issued by the U.S. Treasury. The principal is adjusted to the Consumer Price Index. TIPS are offered in 5-year, 10-year and 20-year maturities.

A **mortgage-backed security** (MBS) is an asset-backed security. The cash flow is backed by the principal and interest payments of mortgages. Payments are typically made monthly. You can have commercial MBS or residential MBS.

Asset-backed securities are bonds based on pools of assets. The financial assets backing the asset-backed securities are related to credit card debt, loans, leases, accounts receivables and royalties.

Most bonds are traded in the OTC market. The OTC market comprises firms and banks that trade bonds. Some dealers trade their inventory of bonds. Other dealers act as agents and trade in response to requests by customers. Bonds sold in this market are usually sold in $5,000 denominations.

The NYSE operates the main bond market in the U.S. It offers investors corporate (including convertibles), agency and government bonds. The NYSE also trades debt and equity structured corporate issues, such as capital securities, retail debt securities, mandatory convertible securities and equity-linked debt securities.

You can find detailed information about bonds available at the NYSE at:

www.nyse.com/productservices/securities/1095449059236.html

On the SIFMA (Securities Industry and Financial Markets Association) site (www.investinginbonds.com/learnmore.asp?catid=5) you can find useful information about investing in bonds.

When investing in bonds you face an interest-rate risk. The relationship between bond prices and interest rates influences your investment. When interest rates decrease, the price will tend to rise. When interest rates rise, the price will tend to fall. The longer the maturity, the bigger the fluctuation of price as interest rates change. For more information see: www.investinginbonds.com/learnmore.asp?catid=3&id=57.

Bond mutual funds do not have a fixed maturity and their price fluctuates in response to changes in interest rates depending on the average portfolio maturity. The credit risk refers to the creditworthiness of the bond issuer and its possibility of default. A prepayment risk refers to the possibility that a bond owner will receive the principal investment back from the issuer prior to the maturity date.

Read about bonds risks at:

www.investinginbonds.com/learnmore.asp?catid=3&id=383

Markets characteristics

Market integrity, flow of information, best execution, transparency

Flow of information available to investors, together with market integrity, transparency and best execution, are attributes related to market quality. Other aspects involve liquidity, the transaction costs, and the speed of execution. They are all very important to ensure that markets work efficiently. Aspects of market architecture, such as the way participants access trading platforms, technology implemented, order types and opening hours also have an influence.

Market integrity aims to ensure a fair and safe operation of financial markets. Confidence is a fundamental prerequisite to attract investments. Regulators focus on issues related to price formation and the prevention of manipulative behaviour. **A sound legal framework is the basis for adequate investor's protection and proper financial practices.**

Valid design of products is key to market integrity based on composition characteristics, such as number and liquidity of components stocks, method of calculation and market structure. Market structure consists of trading rules, information presentation systems and information communications systems (e.g. the trading systems) of a market. It determines what traders know and what they can do. Deep and liquid markets also contribute to integrity. Competitive structures, transaction costs, market infrastructure and diverse market participants are important factors to take into account, together with standardization in trading and settlement practices, transparency of market price and trade information.

Transparency, in particular, is the basis of fair and competitive markets and one of the prerequisites of any efficient market. Investors have confidence in markets that release available market data to the public as they make various uses of this data for trading purposes. There are different degrees to which markets report trading information to the public. Transparent markets quickly report the information available to the public. Ex ante transparent markets quickly report quotes and orders. Ex post transparent markets quickly report trades.

Markets that report only the best bid and offer show the top of the book while markets that report the bid and offer at multiple prices have open limit order books.

Visible bids and offers are available on the market without the identity of the buyer and seller, thus allowing anonymous trading.

Investors may have an interest in anonymity in order to execute trades without letting on their intentions about the securities they are willing to buy or sell. This information, in fact, could generate speculation about the future direction of prices.

Investors need to have a steady and timely flow of information to support their decision whether to buy, sell or hold a specific security. **In fast markets, the timely flow of information to investors is fundamental.**

The disclosure of financial information to the public is required by the SEC to allow the public to make their investment decisions. Market participants can base decisions on the same information reducing price volatility. Comprehensive, accurate information, and effective mechanisms for releasing news is key for investors to have confidence in efficient, and transparent markets, which have the function of attracting capital to develop a nation's economy. Companies are motivated to provide disclosure, as transparency is generally well regarded by markets.

A large number of investors entered equity markets in the past years, performing an important function for the economies. Access to information on a similar basis to large institutions enables the public to develop and maintain confidence in financial markets. The rules to disclose and disseminate price-sensitive information quickly and fairly to the public is important to regulators and it is fundamental to market integrity.

The concept of best execution is related to price but also speed of execution, anonymity, transparency, liquidity, and transactions costs.

The definition of best execution is not so clear and straightforward. Price is one aspect of execution quality while speed of execution is also important to traders. The order type determines which aspect is predominant. In fact, traders who apply market orders are more concerned with speed, while limit-order traders are more concerned with price. Therefore, **best execution does not necessarily mean that customers must receive the best possible price available anywhere in the market.**

Other aspects to consider are those related to internalization, preferencing and order-crossing. Dealers internalize orders when they fill their clients' orders. Brokers preference orders when they route their clients' orders to dealers in exchange for payments for order flow. Brokers can also preference orders when they route their clients' limit orders to ECNs that pay them liquidity fees for orders executed. Brokers cross orders internally when they arrange trades among their clients. These practices bring trades away from organized markets, fragmenting the markets.

Traders and regulators wonder whether these practices comply with the obligation of best execution. For sure, they decrease transparency. Maximizing payment for order flow or profits from internalization may create conflicts of interest for brokers because of their fiduciary obligation of best execution.

Regulators who are engaged in ensuring investor protection address their effort to constantly improve market integrity. The issue of modifying the current asset of Self-Regulatory Organizations is still open and discussed in the U.S.

Electronic trading platforms and other technological innovations introduced in the past years, and that continue to be implemented at a fast pace, improve overall market performance and efficiency.

Direct access and electronic systems provide higher transparency to markets, ensuring speed of execution, anonymity and market integrity. Electronic markets have increased the flow of information available to customers through real-time connectivity. Also, transaction costs and market liquidity benefit from the new environment.

The ongoing process of consolidation and the evolution of market structures with new protocols, order types and opening hours has improved and continues to improve competition and efficiency of markets.

Market hours

Trading takes place in trading sessions. Exchanges are organized either in continuous trading sessions or call-market trading sessions. In the first case, trading occurs at any moment when the market is open with traders that continuously can submit their orders and attempt to execute their trades. Almost all major stock, bonds, futures and options markets are organized in continuous trading sessions. In the second case, trades can be made only when the market is called. Securities may be called simultaneously or in rotation. Call markets focus the traders' interest in a specific security at the same time and at the same place, providing liquidity to the market.

The "trading hours" indicate when the market accepts orders and arranges trades. Usually, markets schedule their trading hours during normal business hours. NYSE, AMEX and NASDAQ open at 09:30 ET and close at 16:00 ET. This allows the submission and collection of orders before the open and the settlement of trades at the end of the session.

Markets often schedule after-hours sessions, where traders can execute their transactions after the end of the business day. During these sessions, liquidity is generally lower and you may experience thin volume. However, under specific situations, for example when earning news is released after the market closure, specific stocks can be very active. As trading develops on a global basis in different markets and continents, many assets can be traded at the same time (for example, in Europe and in the U.S. in several different exchanges at the same time). Tracking quotes in after and pre-market hours in the different markets provides good possibilities to traders, but can also make things more difficult to manage.

Some markets, such as the electronic Globex, provide the possibility to trade assets 24 hours a day. The E-minis can be traded throughout the day from Sunday at 17:45 ET to Friday at 16:15 ET. During the week, the market is closed only between 16:15 ET and 16:30 ET for the daily price settlement. Of course, the night volume is low, but especially in Europe when it is morning (around 03:00 ET), you will see that volume will start increasing. Around 08:00 ET, volume will definitively be higher, providing good liquidity to traders. This allows European traders to operate effectively on U.S. markets and assets.

As you can see in Appendix – Trading Hours (see page 217), exchanges propose very different trading hours for the securities traded. You have to carefully check the market opening hours and the type of platform that supports the trading of a specific security. Also check the possibility to have a call-market auction at the open/close in many continuous order-driven exchanges. In addition to that, some financial instruments may also have simultaneous trading, for example the CBOT agricultural futures contracts, both on the floor and the electronic platform. You might also have the asset traded on the floor during business hours and on the electronic platform during the rest of the day. See the websites of the exchanges to learn about these possibilities. Following the many differences among markets is a complex task, but learning more about the trading hours offered by the exchanges to trade the various assets can also be helpful. In summary, make sure you know exactly in which markets and when you can trade the instrument you are interested in; this knowledge can make the difference.

After-hours trading

Extended-hours trading allows traders to operate before the markets open at 09:30 ET and after the close at 16:00 ET. After-hours trading encompasses transactions that occur after the 16:00 ET regular session close and generally it continues until 20:00 ET. Pre-market trading is related to transactions that occur before the regular session open at 09:30 ET and it is generally conducted from 07:00 ET to 09:30 ET.

Research reports, such as upgrades and downgrades on individual stocks, are usually released in the morning between 07:00 ET and 09:00 ET. Companies typically release their earnings results before 09:00 ET or after 16:00 ET. **Through the extended-hours trading, the average trader has the ability to make trading decisions as soon as the information is disseminated.**

You may want to enter a position to try to anticipate the subsequent move associated to the information released. You can also attempt to open/close a position at better conditions with respect to what was possible during the normal trading hours, placing limit orders.

After-hours trading activity can provide indications about the next day's direction of prices at the open. It can also provide insight about the Asian markets activity as those markets open within hours of the close of the U.S. after-hours market.

In Appendix – Trading Hours (see page 217), you can read about the possibility of trading financial instruments outside normal market hours provided by the exchanges. Make sure you check the trading hours on the exchanges' websites because they may change.

It is amazing how today's average trader can have a global reach to markets at a very limited cost. On electronic platforms you trade seamlessly, submitting the same types of orders virtually 24 hours a day.

Most brokers give you the ability to trade NASDAQ, NYSE and AMEX stocks during extended-hours trading. If you trade stocks, almost all extended-hours trading is processed through ECNs. Trades can be placed the same way as during regular market hours. Traders can place orders of any size within the limits determined by the ECNs. Commissions are normally the same as those applied during regular market hours. Sometimes, an exchange can halt the trading of a stock because of news or other significant events.

Extended-hours trading has some risks to be taken into account. There may be lower liquidity in extended-hours trading compared with regular market hours. Trading is concentrated on few assets, often involved in some news announcement.

In low liquidity conditions, there is the possibility that your orders are not executed or only partially executed. A specific instrument's liquidity influences trading during extended hours and traders can experience wide spreads, with a large difference between the bid and ask. As a result, you may receive an inferior price than you would during regular market hours.

Also because of low liquidity situations, there may be greater volatility in extended-hours trading than in regular market hours; prices can be manipulated and do not reflect the prices either at the end of regular market hours, or upon the opening the next morning.

News announcements, which usually occur during the after hours in low liquidity conditions, may significantly affect prices with the possibility of dealing with spikes.

Check with your broker the validity of the orders you submit. It may happen that orders not executed during the after-hours session are cancelled or they are entered at the open of the regular session. Also check if an order submitted during regular trading hours is still outstanding in the after-hours session.

It is very important to know the market structure of the instrument you want to trade. The knowledge of trading hours, rules and procedures and the orders supported can impact on your trading performance. Knowledge of the market phases and the possibilities you have during each phase might influence your trades.

For example, should you trade futures on the Globex platform, you would have the following phases: Market enabled/pre-opening, pre-opening/No-cancel, (Market Open), continuous trading, (Market Close), and Maintenance Period (see below). In each phase, traders have different possibilities to enter, modify or cancel their orders.

Knowledge of the different phases and the times in which they occur is critical to avoid making mistakes, but also to exploit the specific market structure.

Globex platform, phases graph

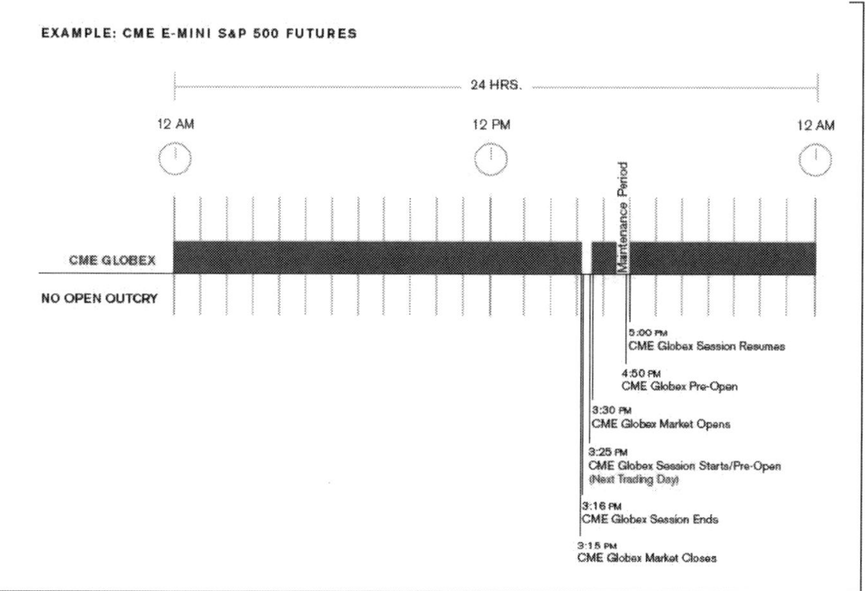

CME E-mini S&P 500 futures graph

	ORDER ENTRY	ORDER MODIFICATION	ORDER CANCELLATION
CME GLOBEX SESSION STARTS			
Market Enabled/Pre-Opening	●	●	●
Pre-Opening/No-Cancel	●	▣	▣
Market Open			
Continuous Trading	●	●	●
Market Close			
Surveillance Intervention	▣	▣	●
CME GLOBEX SESSION ENDS			
Maintenance Period	▣	▣	▣

** Similar trading cycles are used to resume trading after regularly scheduled maintenance or after a system shutdown.*

● Authorized (Action Permissible)   ▣ Blocked (Action Non-Permissible)

For further information about the after-hours trading you can visit:

Understanding the Risks

www.sec.gov/investor/pubs/afterhours.htm

Special Study:

Electronic Communication Networks and After-Hours Trading

Division of Market Regulation

June 2000

www.sec.gov/news/studies/ecnafter.htm

Clearing and settlement

Clearing and settlement are fundamental processes in financial markets. After the trade is executed, the record is submitted to the clearing agency, which matches the buyer and seller record and confirms that the counterparts agree to the terms. The agency reports discrepancies to traders in case the reports do not match, who then try and resolve them. After the clearing process is performed, through settlement, agencies fulfil the delivery requirements of the securities object of a trade.

The settlement agency receives cash from buyers and securities from sellers and, at the end of the process, gives the securities to the buyer and the cash to the seller. Agencies perform an important function in case a trader is not trustworthy or creditworthy.

An important reference to understand the clearing process is the following SEC article:

Clearing Agencies

www.sec.gov/divisions/marketreg/mrclearing.shtml

The article clarifies that clearing agencies are self-regulatory organizations that have to register with the SEC. You can have two types of clearing agencies: clearing corporations and depositories.

"Clearing corporations compare member transactions (or report to members the results of exchange comparison operations), clear those trades and prepare instructions for automated settlement of those trades, and often act as intermediaries in making those settlements. Depositories hold securities certificates in bulk form for their participants and maintain ownership records of the securities on their own books." Depositories hold cash and securities on behalf of their clients and help ensure the security of the clients' assets.

"Clearing corporations, generally, instruct depositories to make securities deliveries that result from settlement of securities transactions. In addition, depositories receive instructions from participants to move securities from one participant's account to another participant's account."

Participants are notified on a daily basis about the securities delivery and payments.

The clearing corporation "guarantees the completion of all transactions and interposes itself as the contraparty to both sides of any transaction." This procedure is fundamental to protect traders when the counterpart of a trade is not trustworthy or creditworthy.

Clearing corporations include:

- National Securities Clearing Corporation (NSCC) (www.nscc.com)

- Fixed Income Clearing Corporation (FICC) (www.ficc.com)

- Options Clearing Corporation (OCC) (www.optionsclearing.com)

Currently, The Depository Trust Company (DTC) is the primary U.S. securities depository.

The Depository Trust Company (https://login.dtcc.com/dtcorg/index.html) is a subsidiary of the Depository Trust & Clearing Corporation (DTCC) (www.dtcc.com). The depository retains custody of some 2 million securities issues. The depository also provides services necessary for the maintenance of the securities it has in custody.

The NSCC, together with the FICC, is a subsidiary of the DTCC. The NSCC provides centralized clearance, settlement and information services for broker-to-broker equity, corporate bond and municipal bond, exchange-traded funds and UIT trades. NSCC generally clears and settles trades on a T+3 basis.

The FICC began operations on January 1, 2003. It is divided into the Government Securities Division and the Mortgage-Backed Securities Division.

The OCC was founded in 1973. It is the largest equity Derivatives Clearing Organization (DCO). It began as a clearinghouse for listed equity options and evolved into an entity that clears a multitude of diverse products. OCC operates under the jurisdiction of both the SEC and the CFTC.

Under its SEC jurisdiction, OCC clears transactions for put and call options on common stocks and other equity issues, stock indexes, foreign currencies, interest-rate composites and single-stock futures. As a registered DCO under CFTC jurisdiction, it provides clearing and settlement services for transactions in futures and options on futures.

OCC's participant exchanges include the AMEX, CBOE, ISE, NYSE Arca, PHLX, and the BSE. OCC also serves markets trading commodity futures, commodity options, and security futures, clearing commodity contracts traded on CBOE Futures Exchange and Philadelphia Board of Trade, respectively, as well as security futures contracts traded on OneChicago.

Futures, options and swap markets have their own clearing house that clears and settles trades in derivatives contracts. Clearing houses are owned by clearing members. Traders must have a clearing member guarantee the settlement of their trades. The clearing house takes responsibility in case of failure in settling a trade by one of the members.

The clearing house maintains the record of trades and settles the margin flow on a daily basis for its clearing member. It acts as the buyer to each seller of a futures contract or other derivative, and as the seller to each buyer and, through settlement, fulfils the delivery requirements.

A derivative instrument is physically settled if the underlier has to be physically delivered in exchange for a specified payment. You have a cash settlement when the underlying instrument is not physically delivered and the transaction ends with a profit or loss.

Some derivatives are cash settled because physical delivery would be impossible. Examples include futures and options contracts for indexes, which cannot be delivered. An interest-rate cap has to be cash settled because the underlying instrument is an interest rate, which cannot be physically delivered.

The settlement date is the date specified for the traded instrument to actually change hands and or be paid, which typically occurs on the same date. A trade is spot settled if the settlement date occurs on a specific date shortly after the trade date, normally one or two business days from trade date. A trade is cash settled if settlement occurs on the trade date and a trade is forward settled if it settles on some date after spot.

Unlike the stock market, futures settle daily. Profits and losses depend on the daily movements of the market, and they are deducted or credited to a person's account each day.

The settlement price is the official price calculated by the exchange at the close of trading to calculate the margin. Settlement prices are used to determine whether gains or losses were made on a given contract. Settlement prices are also required to determine if an investor's margin account requires a margin call.

When a clearing member is long or short at the end of the trading day, settlement shall be made to the settlement price for that day, and such member shall be liable to pay to, or entitled to collect from, the clearing house any loss or profit represented by the difference between the price at which the commodity was bought or sold and the settlement price.

Different formulas are used to calculate the settlement price and they depend on how active trading was during the closing range. Normally, the settlement price is some average of transaction prices immediately before the close of trading (30-60 seconds) or other indicative quote. For example, settlement prices for the E–Mini S&P 500 Stock Price Index Futures, the E–Mini NASDAQ 100 Index Futures, and the E–Mini Currency Futures contract months shall equal the settlement prices for the corresponding contract months of the S&P 500 Stock Price Index Futures, the NASDAQ 100 Index Futures, and the Currency Futures, respectively.

Liquidity

Liquidity is defined as the ability to trade large size quickly at a low cost. It is one of the most important characteristics of a market. Traders should be aware of the liquidity characteristics of a market before approaching it as not doing so could be expensive. A liquid market allows traders to implement their strategies cheaply, normally with a limited bid/ask spread. A liquid market is characterized by high volume. It is generally less volatile than an illiquid market. Market players refer to liquidity in different ways, depending on their perspective. In general, however, liquidity is the object of a bilateral search, where buyers search for sellers and sellers search for buyers. For example, when you find a buyer for your sell order, you have found liquidity. Usually, you can refer to three dimensions of liquidity - time, size and cost:

- **"Immediacy"** refers to how quickly you can execute a trade of a given size at a given cost. When you issue a market order, you are looking for immediacy, although you are not sure that you will be able to satisfy all your requirements in terms of size and cost.

- **Width** refers to the cost of executing a trade of a given size, including commissions. Generally defined also as market breadth, it is the bid/ask spread when you trade a small size.

- **Depth** refers to the size of a trade that can be executed at a given cost.

Width and depth are very strictly related. A liquid market is a market where you can trade large size quickly at low cost.

Depending on whether you are demanding or supplying liquidity to a market, you can have a different cost and/or immediacy. Traders, who demand liquidity issuing market orders, generally make use of exchanges' trading systems that make available who wants to trade at which price. Liquidity suppliers in these markets provide firm quotes and orders. Order-driven trading systems automatically search for the best price using price priority rules. Other traders issue limit orders offering liquidity to the markets. Depending on whether you are a small or a large trader, your problems in exposing your requirements for liquidity is very different. In fact, large traders generally do not want to expose their orders.

Different market players might be willing to offer liquidity to a market. They are arbitrageurs, market makers, block dealers and traders who invest on fundamentals. When a individual trader approaches a market, they have to be aware of the general liquidity conditions of that market. This is because an illiquid market can heavily affect a trading strategy that might have tested well on paper. Results in practice, in this case, can be very different. In fact, an illiquid market usually presents higher costs of trading as the bid/ask spread is large, especially in volatile conditions. It might happen that, asking for immediacy, you have to pay a high cost. Therefore, **unless you have specific interest in illiquid markets, the advice is to trade only liquid markets**. Select the market or asset you want to trade and check the liquidity those specific products offer. For example, should you decide to trade the S&P index, you will find that the E-Mini S&P provides an excellent liquidity where immediacy, depth and width are ensured throughout the trading day.

Even at lunchtime, when trading gets less frenetic, presence on the market of the different players also provides a minimum spread and good depth for not-so-small traders.

If you trade stocks, the size of the company's shares you decide to trade is important. A blue chip develops high trading volume. The liquidity is high and the three dimensions of liquidity are ensured. Therefore, as a trader you can experience a limited bid/ask spread, even if you are willing to buy or sell a large volume of stock.

Penny stocks are far from providing a liquid market. Traders willing to approach this type of market have to be aware of the trading environment they have to face and submit their orders accordingly. Similarly, the after-hours trading on many stocks often presents an illiquid environment.

Volatility

Volatility refers to the tendency of prices to change unexpectedly. Prices change as a response to new information that impacts on the asset value and to the demand of traders who demand liquidity. Volatility can be defined as a measure of an instrument's tendency to move up and down in price over the latest n periods.

Volatility is often expressed using variances, standard deviations or mean absolute deviations of price changes:

- The **variance** is the average squared difference between the price change and the average price change

- The **standard** deviation is the square root of the variance

- The **mean absolute** deviation is the absolute average difference between the price change and the average price change

Volatility changes through time. Markets oscillate between contractions and expansions. When the market moves between areas of equilibrium (the balance of supply and demand), it does so quickly through range expansions. Markets typically move by alternating between trends and congestions. Statistics say that markets spend longer periods of time developing congestions and trading ranges than trends. The move to new areas of balance is then fast and usually short. Markets oscillate between expansions and contractions in a cyclical rhythm. Volatility, risk and profit are closely related. Traders must be aware of the potential effects of volatility on their positions. Option traders are especially concerned with volatility. Option contract values depend heavily on the volatility of the underlying instrument. Option traders must be able to measure and try to "predict" volatility to trade profitably. Volumes and volatility are often correlated, although their relationship is not simple.

It is also true that every market displays a different "market personality." The average daily range provides a powerful insight into the personality of a market. It helps measure the activity of the market players and how easily prices manage to move on a daily basis. By observing the behaviour of prices, you gain an understanding of the underlying asset and the characteristics of the market players. The average daily range, expressed as a percentage, can be defined as a ratio between the average true range (length) and the average of the last n daily closes. It gives an idea of how quickly a market is able to move between areas of price balance. It is generally low in bonds ($\leq 1\%$) and currency markets. It is higher in stock index futures and in some commodities. The daily range normally expands in the direction of the trend and contracts during reactions, although you will sometimes notice significant divergences.

Instruments that experience wider daily trading ranges (e.g. stocks and futures) are considered more volatile and more risky. Some traders, especially day traders, prefer volatile instruments because the cost of trading (commission fees, for example) is the same, yet the potential for a profit can be greater. Of course, the risk for loss is also greater.

Volatility is important to regulators. High volatility indicates the possibility that markets are not functioning well. Volatility can be expressed as a combination of a fundamental and transitory component. Fundamental volatility is generated by unexpected changes in instrument values. New information can impact on fundamental values of instruments. Expected changes and expected events usually do not change prices significantly. Transitory volatility is generated by impatient traders and prices, in this case, that diverge from their fundamentals in the short term. Eventually they revert to fundamental values. Transitory volatility is also related to the bid/ask spread and is small in liquid markets. The distinction is important both for traders and regulators. Regulators can affect transitory volatility, but cannot do much about fundamental volatility as they try to create liquid markets that produce highly informative prices.

Volatility is very relevant to option traders. Often, traders will find the following categorization and description of volatility:

- **Historic volatility** is a measure of price changes during a specific time period in the past

- **Future volatility** represents, for example, the standard deviation of daily returns in a given future period. Option pricing formulas need it as an input to calculate the theoretical value of an option. However, future volatility can only be an estimate.

- **Expected volatility** is a forecast of volatility used in an option pricing formula to estimate the theoretical value of an option

- **Implied volatility** is the volatility that explains the current market price of an option. The terms overvalued and undervalued for a price of an option are related to the relationship between implied volatility and expected volatility.

A popular measure of implied volatility in index options is CBOE's Volatility Index (www.cboe.com/micro/vix/introduction.aspx), (ticker symbol VIX).

The VIX is a measure of the implied volatility of a range of options based on the S&P 500. It reflects investors' assessment of near-term market volatility, or risk. If implied volatility is high, the premium on options will be high and will reflect rising expectation of future volatility of the stock index. Generally, it is believed that a high VIX displays increased investor fear and a low VIX suggests complacency. Historically, this pattern in the relationship between the VIX and the stock market has repeated itself in bull and bear cycles. During bear market periods, the VIX spiked higher, reflecting the high demand for puts as a hedge against declines. During bullish periods, there is less need for portfolio managers to purchase puts. Many traders use the VIX as a contrarian tool in attempting to pinpoint market tops and bottoms.

PART II:

Mechanics – Brokers, Accounts and Information Sources

Brokers

Brokers

Brokers are agents who arrange trades for their clients. Unlike dealers, who trade with their clients, brokers trade their clients' orders. A broker is broadly defined as any person engaged in the business of effecting transactions in securities for the account of others. For instance, a person who executes transactions for others on a securities exchange is a broker.

> The role of the broker:
>
> - Arrange for dealers to fill their clients' orders
> - Match their clients' buy and sell orders
> - Introduce their clients to electronic trading systems
> - Are paid commissions for their services
> - Are also often financial advisers and can provide financial information

By law, securities firms doing business with the American public must register with the National Association of Securities Dealers (NASD). NASD write rules to govern their behaviour, examine them for compliance, and enforce actions when rules are broken (www.finra.org/RulesRegulation/index.htm).

Brokers and dealers must register with the SEC and join a self-regulatory organization (SRO).

You can read the following guide at the SEC website:

Guide to Broker-Dealer Registration

Division of Market Regulation

U.S. Securities and Exchange Commission

December 2005

www.sec.gov/divisions/marketreg/bdguide.htm#I

Different from brokers, dealers buy and sell securities for their own accounts, adding liquidity to the marketplace and seeking to profit from the spread between the prices at which they buy and sell. In the OTC market, dealers often provide the bid and ask quotes of a security, committing their capital to securities, which they are ready to trade at the quoted prices.

Finding a broker and opening an account with a broker is easy. What is complex is identifying the broker that exactly matches your needs. You have a variety of brokerage firms to choose from. The issue is that you have to know what you require in terms of services offered, products traded and exchanges where you want to trade. Commissions, quality of execution, reliability and support are only some of the features you have to take into account.

Let's analyze the items you might want to consider in the process of selecting your broker:

- **Minimum account size**. Normally, the account size requested for futures, stocks and options is different and it has to be verified on a case-by-case basis. The advice is that you do not start trading being undercapitalized, especially in the futures markets, as it might lead to margin calls and difficult situations.

- **Commissions**. Usually, commission rates are different for every type of product. If you are an active trader, brokers often have programs that reduce commissions in accordance with volume or number of round turn trades executed.

- **Trading margins** are to be considered, keeping in mind the leverage associated to the use of margins. Lower margins allow speculative positions, but increase your overall risk exposure.

- **Services offered**. There is a great variety of services offered to choose from. Very much depends on what you require. Brokers often offer services about technical and fundamental analysis, charts and graphs, trading software (in order to create trading systems, scan and sort securities based on various criteria), headline news, portfolio management, wireless connectivity (to quotes, alerts, execution) and so forth. They can often provide clients with high-speed, direct-access trading platforms, with real-time quotes and point-and-click execution. The offer can also include simulated trading platforms for clients' training and testing purposes. Trading from Europe, it is important to verify the availability of a 24 hour technical support and customer service with a trading center to place orders and request support by telephone means. This is important in case you experience network problems or if your computer crashes. Many brokers also offer systems trading and managed account programs.

- **Type of Account**. The type of account to open has to be studied carefully depending on the assets you want to trade and the services you need. For example, you can consider a Full Service Broker, a Discount Broker or a Deep Discount Broker. Brokers propose different accounts for equities, futures, options and currencies.

- **Execution method**. For example, through electronic direct-access trading by scanning market makers, ECNs, exchanges, and hidden pools of liquidity for the best available execution, or a trade desk designed to meet clients' needs when they call to place trades over the phone. Or both with multiple backup order-entry systems in case of an outage of the main systems.

- Verify that the broker covers the exchanges of interest to you. Examples might be CBOT, CME, NYSE, NASDAQ, AMEX.

- The type of orders supported by the broker might be of interest to you if you require specific order instructions to be executed in order to apply your trading strategies. Stop, limit, stop limit, market orders are normally offered by every broker. More specific instructions, however, have to be verified.

It is important to note that in order to trade U.S. markets, it is not necessary to open an account in the U.S. There are many European brokers that allow access to U.S. markets, providing excellent service and comparable commission plans and fees. This particular choice has to be made taking into consideration all the above mentioned elements. There are brokers that have access on global markets, giving an ample range of choices to traders.

Let's now see the types of typical retail brokers in the U.S. markets. Brokers differ in the relationship they have with their clients and the services provided. Commissions, therefore, vary according to these parameters and the instruments traded. Instruments offered generally include:

- Stocks

- Options

- Treasury bills

- Notes and bonds

- ETFs

- Mutual funds

- Futures contracts

- **Deep Discount Brokers**. Typically, clients submit their orders via the internet. These brokers provide very limited investment information resources and research. They do not provide investment or financial planning services. You can normally find firms with no physical offices or, as an alternative, online branches of full-service/discount firms. Virtual firms offer the cheapest commissions and fees. Online firms, besides providing 24-hour access to your account, offer the possibility to do research, manage your portfolio and read market news, but they offer no personal advice or point of contact.

- **Discount Brokers**. Clients have the capability to submit orders over the phone or at a discount via the internet. Sometimes, clients may be offered access to investment research and financial information, and stock reports or some fee-based investment planning service.

- **Full-Service Brokers**. These develop a personal relationship with their clients, where clients trust their brokers. Brokers, typically, provide investment research, and investment and financial planning services. Directed account trading is available. Often, retail full-service accounts are on a periodical fee basis.

You can find different ways of categorizing brokers. As time passes, it is difficult to say what services are provided by discount or deep discount brokers. The effect of competition is bringing more and more services to clients. Commissions for the different types of brokers vary substantially.

They also change frequently because competition is high. There is a tendency, however, to offer more services keeping the same level of commissions.

It is not uncommon for brokers in the financial-services industry to change firms. When this occurs, investors have to make up their mind whether or not they move to the new firm with their broker. Although a good relationship with a broker is important, investors should protect their interests to be sure they are making a well informed decision.

For more information see:
www.nyse.com/pdfs/your_broker_changes_firms.pdf

At www.smartmoney.com/brokers/index.cfm?story=august2006, you can read the results of a survey conducted by SmartMoney.com in July 2006. The survey investigated customer services, trading tools, banking services, investment products, research, and the offer of mutual funds as elements to consider for discount brokers. Statements, trust, customer satisfaction and stock picking were considered for full-service brokers. It is very interesting and indicative of firms and services offered, but I would not take the results for granted. The environment is so dynamic and competitive that things can change very quickly.

Interesting resources:

Protect Your Money:

Tips for Checking Out Brokers and Investment Advisers

www.sec.gov/investor/brokers.htm

www.sec.gov/divisions/marketreg/bdguide.htm

Investment advisers provide advice about investing in securities. Investment advisers who manage $25 million or more generally must register with the SEC. If they manage less, they generally must register with their state securities agency.

You can view an adviser's registration status online by visiting the Investment Adviser Public Disclosure (IAPD) website at: www.adviserinfo.sec.gov/IAPD/Content/IapdMain/iapd_SiteMap.aspx.

As of today, the database contains information only for those who register electronically using the IARD www.sec.gov/divisions/investment/iard.shtml.

In the future, the database will expand to encompass all registered investment advisers in every state.

Used to find information about brokers and brokerage firms, the Central Registration Depository (CRD) (www.sec.gov/answers/crd.htm) is a database that allows you to see whether brokers are properly licensed, and whether they have had run-ins with regulators or have received serious complaints from investors. You can ask your state securities regulator or FINRA to provide you with information from the CRD.

At the FINRA website (http://www.finra.org/InvestorInformation/InvestorProtection/ChecktheBackgroundofYourInvestmentProfessional/index.htm) you can check the professional background of current and former registered firms and brokers using the FINRA BrokerCheck tool. It is a free online tool, which is important when choosing whether to do business with a particular broker or brokerage firm. The FINRA BrokerCheck allows the search of both a broker and brokerage firm, and the online delivery of a related report. It also provides explanations to help investors better understand the information provided.

Once you've checked out the registration and record of your financial professional or firm, you can also check whether the brokerage firm and its clearing firm are members of the Securities Investor Protection Corporation (SIPC) (www.sipc.org).

SIPC can provide customer protection if a brokerage firm becomes insolvent. However, it will not be able to intervene if you've opened an account with a non-SIPC member and the firm goes out of business.

See the Barrons' *Tools of the Trade* article to read about an interesting survey of the brokers available at: http://webreprints.djreprints.com/1664971178338.html and the table at: http://webreprints.djreprints.com/barronsbroker-final2.pdf.

Direct-access trading vs. online trading vs. traditional broker-directed trading

There are three ways you can decide to conduct your trading activity:

1. Online trading using the internet and a web-based broker

2. Direct-access trading (DAT)

3. Traditional broker services

When using the services of an online broker, a client logs on to the broker's website and places orders through the internet browser. Before the order is executed several intermediaries may be involved and some time may be needed for the order to be processed and sent to the marketplace. Many online firms, in fact, do not always execute orders directly and may send orders to others to execute. A broker has different ways for executing orders. A broker may attempt to fill an order by sending it to the floor of the exchange (for example the NYSE or a regional exchange in case of a stock). What is known as "payment for order flow" may be the reason for some routing alternative. The order may go to a third market maker in case the broker is not a member of the exchange where the stock is listed. The order may be internalized when the broker decides to fill your order from the inventory of stocks the firm owns. In markets such as NASDAQ, the order may go to a specific market maker as the broker may make a profit by sending orders to certain market makers. In summary, as the order is routed according to the different logics, this could result both in slow execution and orders filled at higher prices. When speed of execution is a requirement, online brokerage firms are not appropriate. If, for example, you are a momentum trader and you normally use market orders, you might find online trading unsatisfactory and expensive because of slow execution and slippage. On the other hand, if you do not have speed requirements and you trade using limit orders, online brokers might be appropriate as you can obtain low commissions.

Scalpers and day traders will find DAT more adapt to meet their requirements. Direct-access describes the ability of individual traders to select to which specific marketplace they route their orders (e.g. ECN, market maker or exchange). These systems allow you to trade stocks or other instruments directly with a market maker or a specialist on the floor of the exchange, or immediate order execution, which is not possible using a conventional online broker.

In today's fragmented market, stocks can be simultaneously quoted in multiple locations at different prices. DAT platforms enable a trader to decide where to route orders to obtain the best price and/or the fastest execution. All order-routing decisions are handled on an order-by-order basis in a completely unbiased fashion, making sure that your orders are not "sold" to market makers.

These systems use proprietary platforms and high-speed connections, that make "real time" trading possible at low cost. Fees are usually required to use the firm's proprietary trading software or platform. Most firms, however, will waive the fee if you make a minimum number of trades per month. From home, you can trade almost as a professional as trading platforms evolve and become more and more sophisticated. There is no-one involved between the stock exchange or ECN and the trader. The speed of the connection from home to the system and the speed of the system itself to manage your trade, however, might still be an issue if you intend to apply sophisticated scalping algorithmic trading or simply automated trading strategies.

Day traders, scalpers and momentum traders use these type of firms because they trade a lot and need discounts on commissions and fees while having speed of execution and lower slippage. Not all order-execution systems are equivalent. There is a significant variety in speed and accuracy of execution among the systems on the market, as well as in commissions charged. As a result, traders have to consider the system that meets their needs in terms of performance, speed and price.

As an example, Level I provides real-time bid/ask quotes for securities trading on the NASDAQ. This type of access doesn't show you the order sizes and does not disclose who is bidding/asking for the stock. On the contrary, with Level II traders have access in "real time" to names and quotations of the market makers and their bid/ask lots. Traders can decide with only one click at which price to place the order and with which market maker to start their trade. The only other decision to make is the number of shares for the order.

When trading through an ECN, orders are executed directly from the trader's DAT and transmitted electronically almost instantaneously to the ECN trading platform.

Traditional brokers establish a personal relationship with their clients. In this case, trust and customer satisfaction are important. Investors that need research and investment and financial planning services will find a great benefit from this type of access to markets. Inactive traders, investors who do not have a specific knowledge of the markets' mechanisms, will find traditional brokers the best solution for their needs. Also, investors who have big capitals to invest and intend to exploit the brokers' experience and competence to manage their portfolios will prefer to pay higher fees and commissions for their trades in exchange for better services. In this case, the speed of execution is not so important as the added value that the broker can provide. Large orders or big positions that need to be built without possibly impacting on price may find application through the broker's implementation capability.

Software platforms

Trading software can help experienced traders, but also beginners, to evaluate and implement their strategies into the marketplace. There are many software platforms available on the market. Often, brokers offer various platforms when you open an account. Some of them may require the payment of a fee, while others, usually less sophisticated, can be provided for free. As an alternative, you can purchase specific applications able to integrate data feeds from different vendors and brokers to execute your orders. The most common platforms, however, share basic characteristics regardless of the logics and technologies implemented. They allow the definition of trading rules and criteria. The software will then scan and find very quickly stocks or other instruments that match your criteria and setups for investment opportunities. The software will then signal buy and sell setups. **You can program your software to place orders automatically, according to your trading rules, or they can be executed manually.** The software will allow you to build a report of your trades and analyze your trading performance. Generally, you will be able to access a range of markets and a historical database to conduct testing activities.

Of course, a software platform cannot suggest the trading style you should apply, but it is an excellent support to make your trading more systematic.

Before you decide to use a software platform to automatically place buy-and-sell orders, the advice is that you get familiar with the market structure, including the type of orders available, hours of operations of the exchange and characteristics of the product you want to trade (options, futures, stocks and so forth).

A software platform can substantially support your activity as a trader/investor. The most important thing, in my opinion, is that it can help you follow the rules that you have established and systematically implement your trading criteria. In fact, lack of control of emotions and discipline is one of the reasons why traders lose money.

There are various types of software on the market with different prices and characteristics. Some are solely for testing and others are for both testing and trading.

If you trade short term-patterns or options, a software platform is a necessity. Of course, there are a lot of trading strategies and techniques on the market. You can find software-based neural networks, artificial intelligence, traditional technical analysis, candlestick pattern, Fibonacci, Gann, Elliot waves, and many others. Sometimes it is not easy for the average investor to choose among so many products. Producers' websites often offer demos that you can use. Magazines and forums report comments about the different software platforms and their characteristics.

For the small trader, the key in choosing a testing and trading platform is to choose a platform that pushes all the historical data. It's one less thing to think about. Moreover, the possibility to program your strategy and test it over a past range of data and markets is also helpful.

Testing is important because it helps traders to approach markets and trading ideas in a scientific manner. By testing, traders can verify how a trading idea has worked in the past and is likely to perform in the future.

Markets change continuously – players may change, the underlying security fundamentals may change and the market structure (rules, procedures and technology of the exchange) may change. In this ever-changing environment, traders need to recognize that a cycle has changed. Discretionary traders trade based on their feelings, while many apply some type of rule when implementing their trading plan. Mechanical traders program their rules and let the computer run the trade or they add some discretion when it comes to implementing their strategy in the real trading environment. Nonetheless, the support of a software tool to test their trading ideas can be very useful to both types of traders.

Some of the platforms use specific dedicated languages to code trading strategies and new indicators that traders build. Although these languages can be quite powerful, sometimes this can be difficult for beginners and much effort is required to learn how to program.

Testing presents some pitfalls and it is not the holy grail of trading. In fact, when testing, you need to take into account slippage, commissions, bad fills and curve-fitting. Most testing platforms have features to deduct slippage and commissions. Slippage occurs when you are filled at the ask instead of the bid. Commissions can impact heavily on a system. Bad fills have to take into account the fact that when you apply limit orders in your system, tests will always show the order as filled, even if only one trade occurred at that price in the marketplace. **Applying limit trading in testing will always provide better results than in the real world.** This is the most insidious issue. In fact, it is very difficult to assess the impact of bad fills on the profitability of the system.

Curve-fitting occurs when rules are added to the basic trading idea to eliminate bad trades. Over-optimization of parameters can similarly provide apparent excellent results, but systems built in this way will never survive the test of time.

There are specific techniques to test systems using out of sample data. This is required to make sure you have not over-optimized the system under test and verify the validity of the system's logic using different sets of data.

Software platforms provide the capability to build strategy performance reports. Sometimes these reports may be complex to understand. They indicate a number of elements to consider when evaluating a strategy.

Net profit enables you to check whether the strategy is eventually profitable. Having a high percentage of winners and a low win/loss ratio may indicate that your system is not satisfactory. You would have to increase the win/loss ratio, likely at the expense of the percentage of winners.

In particular, you have to try to have a good ratio of the average size of winners and losers. The profit factor is probably the most important number and it represents the gross profit divided by gross loss. The higher the number, the better the system. A profit factor of 2 is considered good. Also check the drawdown of the system. It indicates the magnitude of a decline in equity, as measured from a peak to the subsequent trough, and provides you with the assessment of your system's equity volatility. The lower the drawdown the more stable and constant the performance of the system.

Make sure you understand how to read the performance reports or you might come to wrong conclusions when evaluating a strategy.

At Appendix – Software platforms (see page 205) you can find some of the most popular platforms to help you select the most suitable ones for your trading style and technique.

Your account

Open an account – Legal requirements – Funding your account

In this section I approach the steps to opening an account with a U.S. broker. If you live in Europe, nothing prevents you from trading U.S. markets through a European broker, and the same would apply to Asian investors and traders.

However, I think it is interesting to explore the different possibilities available in the U.S. and the requirements to operate establishing an account there, also as a non-resident.

Opening an account with a U.S broker is quite easy and requires little time – just the time to do the paperwork, send the necessary forms and transfer the money. In total, it could take around 7 to 10 days.

When you contact a broker showing your interest in opening an account, the first thing the firm representative will likely do is ask the following questions from their "Compliance Department" related to international clients wanting to open an account:

1. What is your country of citizenship and residency?

2. Do you spend long periods of time in the U.S.? If so, about how long?

3. How did you hear about our brokerage services?

4. Do you have any trading accounts in the U.S.? If so, at which brokerage firms?

5. What do you trade? Stocks, futures, forex, options?

6. If you were to open an account, how much would you be transferring to us and where would you be transferring it from?

7. Please send me your full mailing address and phone number so we can enter your information into our database.

8. What account type are you interested in opening?

In general, there are a number of types of accounts available:

- **Individual**: a personal account in the name of the individual who owns the account. Likely, you would want to open this type of account as a non-U.S. person.

- **Tenants in Common**: an account owned by two or more individuals. If one dies, his or her portion of the account is transferred to his or her designated beneficiary(ies).

- **Joint Tenants with Right of Survivorship**: an account owned by two or more individuals. If one dies, his or her interest in the account automatically passes to the survivor(s) at the time of death.

- **IRA**: an individual retirement account (only for U.S. taxpayers).

- **Roth IRA**: a specific type of individual retirement account created by the Taxpayer Relief Act of 1997 (only for U.S. taxpayers).

- **SEP IRA**: a Simplified Employee Pension (SEP), IRA is a written arrangement where employers make contributions to traditional IRAs set up for employees (only for U.S. taxpayers).

- **Corporation**: an account owned by a corporation.

- **Partnership**: an account owned by a partnership. The account must be in the full, legal name of the partnership.

- **Limited Liability Company**: an account owned by a limited liability company. The account must be in the full, legal name of the limited liability company.

- **Sole Proprietorship**: a business owned by one individual and conducted under a company name.

- **Trust**: a legal entity created by a grantor for the benefit of designated beneficiaries. Trusts are creatures of state law and that law varies from state to state. Accounts opened by a trust must be in the name of the trust.

To open an account you are required to fill out, sign and submit an "Account Agreement". Additional forms and agreements may be required based on the account type and the services you choose. You might require to use the software and data services provided by the broker.

Then you have to subscribe and pay monthly fees to the broker for the use of its platform and exchange fees in case you are interested in real-time data. The platform fee can sometimes be waived if you hit certain trading thresholds or it can be offered for free.

To open an account a broker could ask you to meet the following minimum requirements:

- Annual net income of at least $50,000 and liquid net worth of at least $75,000

- At least 2 years of active trading experience

- Minimum initial equities account balance: $30,000 for Pattern Day Trading Accounts, $10,000 for Non-Day Trading Accounts

- Minimum initial futures or forex account balance of $5,000

- Minimum initial futures or forex IRA account balance of $10,000

- Ability to use risk capital of at least $50,000

A **pattern day trader** is defined as any customer who executes at least 4 day trades of the same security in a 5-trading-day period.

Pattern day traders must maintain at least $25,000 in their accounts and can only trade in margin accounts."

If the account balance falls below $25,000, trading is restricted to closing transactions only until the account balance is increased to $25,000.

For more details see:

Day Trading

www.sec.gov/answers/daytrading.htm

www.patterndaytraderrule.com/patterndaytrader.html

http://en.wikipedia.org/wiki/Pattern_day_trader

Day Trading Margin Requirements: Know the Rules

http://www.finra.org/InvestorInformation/InvestmentChoices/DayTradingInformation/p005906

Non-Day Trading Accounts (an account that has never placed 4 day trades in a 5-trading-day period) must maintain a minimum daily equity balance of at least $5,000.

When trading equities and options, you can typically have two types of accounts:

1. **Cash account**. The customer pays the full purchase price of the stock

2. **Margin account**. The customer pays a portion of the purchase price, the margin, and borrows the balance of the purchase price from the broker.

Margin accounts have many advantages, but you must be aware that there is a higher potential for loss when purchasing stock on margin versus purchasing stock for cash.

When you open an account, you can give another person trading privileges on your account by submitting a third-party trading authorization form to the broker.

Generally, only equities accounts earn interest, and often in excess of specific amounts (e.g. $10,000). To give you an idea, at the time this book was written, for accounts less than $250,000 the equity credit interest rate offered was on average 1.25%. On the other hand, the equity margin rate was 8.25%. However, these rates can change depending on the broker you choose and the market interest rates; I indicated them only as an example and a reference.

The process to open and fund an account with a U.S. broker for a non-U.S. trader would typically be as the following example describes.

You should fill out the account forms provided by the broker, most of the time on its website, and send them to the firm. Once the broker receives the originals back, it takes about 24 hours to get an approved account number. They will then call you with the new account number so you can wire the funds. You can trade the day after the broker receives the funds. They do not e-mail the account number for security reasons. Your account information is then updated in real-time, tick-by-tick.

The fastest way to have funds deposited to your brokerage account is by transferring money electronically (e.g. a wire transfer) from your bank account. For a wire transfer from Europe, you must allow more than a week to have the funds credited. You have to pay attention not to wire funds until your account is approved, and you have to confirm that the account is ready to receive a wire. Normally, you can wire both U.S. and foreign currency. The transfer will be made to a bank account indicated by your broker, for credit to the Customer Segregated Account. For example, on the wiring instructions, you might indicate "Account Number XXX" for further credit to your account name and your account number.

You may send a check via mail along with your signed account documents. Funds are available for withdrawal after a given number of business days (e.g. 10). Brokers, generally, do not accept funding via cash, third-party checks or money orders.

Be aware that opening and maintaining an account is not possible in all jurisdictions. It is possible that the country in which you are a resident prohibits a broker from opening and maintaining an account for you. If in doubt, please contact the broker's account representative. For European traders, however, this should not be an issue.

Trading in futures and options is not appropriate for everybody. Therefore, the Commodity Futures Trading Commission (CFTC) requires that brokers provide their customers with a disclosure document that describes the risks involved in entering into futures and option contracts. You then have the opportunity to consider whether futures and options are appropriate for you. Your experience, objectives and financial resources are elements to take into account. When you open an account, you will find a form that you're to sign to acknowledge that you have been made aware of the risks by your broker.

Tax

As an international customer, you have to know about the tax implications of opening an account in the U.S. and this depends on if you can be classified as a resident alien or a non-resident alien. For tax purposes, an alien is an individual who is not a U.S. citizen. To be considered a resident alien for tax purposes, you must be a non-U.S. citizen who holds a green card or was physically present in the U.S. 31 days during the current year and, according to the U.S. Internal Revenue Service, "183 days during the 3-year period that includes the current year and the 2 years immediately before that, including:

- All the days you were present in the current year.

- 1/3 of the days you were present in the first year before the current year.

- 1/6 of the days you were present in the second year before the current year."

Even if you meet the above requirements "you can be treated as a non-resident alien if:

- You are present in the U.S. for less than 183 days in the year

- Maintain a tax home in a foreign country during the year

- Have a closer connection during the year to a foreign country in which you have a tax home than to the United States"

"A resident alien's income is generally subject to tax in the same manner as a U.S. citizen. If you are a resident alien, you must report all interest, dividends, wages, or other compensation for services, income from rental property or royalties, and other types of income on your U.S. tax return. You must report these amounts whether from sources within or outside the U.S. "

"A non-resident alien usually is subject to U.S. income tax only on U.S. source income. Under limited circumstances, certain foreign source income is subject to U.S. tax."

If a tax treaty between the United States and your country provides an exemption from, or a reduced rate of, tax for certain items of income, you should notify the payer of the income (the withholding agent) of your foreign status to claim a tax treaty withholding exemption. Generally, you do this by filing the form W-8BEN (Certificate of Foreign Status of Beneficial Owner for United States Tax Withholding). When you open an account, as an international customer, the broker will ask you to fill in the W8-BEN form (www.irs.gov/pub/irs-pdf/fw8ben.pdf).

As a non-resident alien, if the only business you have in the U.S. is in trading stocks, securities or commodities, including hedging transactions through a U.S. resident broker or other agent in terms of capital gains, you are not subject to a U.S. capital gains tax, and no money will be withheld by the brokerage firm. You will likely need to pay capital gains tax in your country of origin.

In most cases, dividend income received from domestic corporations is U.S. source income while dividend income from foreign corporations is usually foreign source income.

Non-resident aliens face a tax rate of 30% on dividends paid out by U.S. companies. Dividends, interest-related dividends or short-term capital gain dividends paid by foreign companies are exempt from the 30% tax. This 30%

rate can also be lower depending on the treaty between your home country and the U.S.

U.S. source interest income is considered interest on bonds, notes, or other interest-bearing obligations of U.S. residents or domestic corporations. Non-resident aliens can exclude the interest income from their gross income if they have furnished the payer of the interest or the withholding agent a statement that you are not a U.S. person (form W-8BEN).

For more information, see IRS Publication 519: *U.S. Tax Guide For Aliens*.

United States Department of the Treasury

www.irs.gov/pub/irs-pdf/p519.pdf

United States Department of the Treasury – Publication 901

www.irs.gov/publications/p901/ar02.html#d0e154

Commissions and fees

The costs associated with trading can have a significant impact on returns. That is why traders and investors have to consider these aspects carefully.

Trading costs can be categorized as:

- Explicit costs, such as commissions, fees and taxes

- Bid/ask spread

You can also refer to market-impact costs when a large order is placed on the market that influences price and to opportunity costs associated with waiting to execute a trade.

Explicit costs can be quite high and significant, especially if you are a short-term trader. They can represent a high percentage of your average win trade. In this case, commissions have to be compressed as much as possible, keeping in account your requirement of level of service provided by the broker. In fact, **the brokerage with the lowest commissions is not necessarily the best one for you**. Generally, you get what you pay for. It is a balance that has to be searched between costs and benefits. Reliability, speed of execution and platforms offered have a cost that, as a trader, you have to be ready to accept.

On the other hand, fees cannot be compressed. Exchange fees, regulatory and overnight fees (in case of futures contracts) and others are fixed and you have to pay them to access, for example, real-time data feeds or simply as a per trade cost.

Overtrading brings traders to execute an excessively high number of transactions. Commissions eat up profits quickly and eventually the "system" – brokers and exchanges – are the only ones who earn when you trade. Increasing your average trade profit allows your commissions and fees to be small percentage of your average trade and not impact too much on your returns. Scalpers and day traders follow a different approach based on very frequent trades to catch mean reversion or short-term trend following moves. Low commissions are essential for success given the very small margin they have to make a profit.

As an example, a tick on the E-Mini S&P is worth $12.5. A scalper making 1 tick would realize a profit of $7.5 supposing a $5 round turn commission and fees. It would represent 40% of the gain. Making 2 ticks ($25) would allow the trader to lower the percentage to 20%, which is still a lot. A 4 ticks trade ($50) would lower the weight of commissions to 10%.

It is quite difficult to compare the commissions proposed by the various brokers. Brokers often have different commission plans that depend on many factors. These may include:

- **Account size**: the higher the account balance the lower the commissions might be.

- **Product**: commissions may be lower with one broker for some products and more expensive for others.

- **Trade size**: depending on the number of trades or the size of a trade, brokers may apply a scaled-down commission plan.

- **Type of order**: limit and market orders may be charged differently.

- **Method of execution**: if the order is entered online, the broker will charge lower commissions than for broker-assisted trades. Similarly, different trading platforms (web-based vs. software-based) might have different commission plans.

When you open an account, do not only consider the explicit costs. There are also hidden fees. These may include:

- Inactivity fees that you have to pay if you don't execute a specified number of trades on your account during a set time period

- Transfer fees meant to discourage you from changing brokers

- Account maintenance and activity fees

- Minimum equity requirement fees charged by some brokers when their clients don't maintain a minimum balance of cash and securities

Another aspect is related to the interest that is paid by the broker on your account cash balance. For example, discount brokers allow you to purchase securities paying a low commission per trade. However, the interest paid on the cash balance is usually not competitive (usually between 0.1% and 3%) with what you can get from other brokers or online banks. The interest may also be paid incrementally on the cash balance. In general, keeping cash at the brokerage, if you are not an active trader, does not make your money work as it should. Brokers make profits reinvesting the idle cash of their clients. If regulators don't show interest on the issue, the brokers will not be brought to change their policies. Some brokers allow their clients to sweep excess cash into money-market funds or a savings account.

For more information, you can read a report called "The Cash Sweep Account: What Deal Are You Getting?" from the NYSE at:

www.nyse.com/pdfs/informedinvestor1.pdf

When opening an equities margin account, on the one hand, you do not have to keep your money idle in your account. On the other hand, you pay margin interests, which may also be high (between 7% and 11% in 2007). Futures accounts, usually, are not remunerated.

It is quite difficult to draft a map of commissions for the different types of accounts and the number of products and instruments on the market. When trading futures, commissions may be in the range of $.25-$4 and more in the case of full-service brokers for electronically traded contracts, and up to $7 and more for pit-traded contracts.

When you execute a trade on a futures contract, for example the E-Mini S&P, this is an example of what you could find in your daily statement:

COMMISSION	1.20DR
EXCHANGE & CLEARING FEE	1.14DR
NFA FEE	.01DR
TOTAL COMMISSIONS & FEES	2.35DR

In this case, you can see that the exchange and clearing fee plus the NFA fee impact significantly on the total commissions you are going to pay. This cost cannot be compressed by choosing a different broker.

In the case of futures contracts, take into account that you also have overnight fees if applicable.

Read below an example of what you would be charged in some cases:

- CBOT Non-Exchange Members have to pay exchange fees (0.56-1.81) and regulatory fees (0.01)

- CME Non-Exchange Members have to pay exchange fees (1.14-2.03) and regulatory fees (0.01)

- NYMEX Non-Exchange Members have to pay exchange fees (0.50-1.45) and regulatory fees (0.01)

- OneChicago Non-Exchange Members have to pay exchange fees (0.14-0.50) and regulatory fees (0.01)

All exchange and regulatory fees are provided for informational purposes only and are subject to change by the exchanges.

When trading stocks, commissions vary a lot depending on the type of broker, size of the order, type of order, account balance, etc. It is very difficult to track and compare the brokers' commissions because the commissions, plans and the services offered change continuously, pushed by competition, marketing policies and technological innovation.

Generally speaking, you can usually find commissions ranging from $5 to $20. Brokers may offer either a flat commission, regardless of the number of shares object of the trade, or charge a commission based on the number of shares bought/sold. Depending on the size of your typical trade, you may find one type of plan or the other.

You can also find plans where commissions decrease with the size of the trade or facilitate the execution of scaling in/out of positions.

The same concepts apply to options, where commissions may vary, generally, between $5 and $20 and depend mostly on the number of contracts object of the trade.

Some firms may offer reduced commissions or waive fees, related for instance to inactivity or maintenance fees, or provide additional services, if certain account-activity and/or specified account-balance criteria are met. Commissions on bonds and mutual funds are also variable. You can easily expect to be charged from $15 to $75.

Online access to your account

Individual traders and investors, almost in the totality of cases, require online access to their accounts to execute their trades, check their balance, manage their portfolio and enjoy the services offered by their brokers.

This is very easy to do; it provides a lot of benefits and flexibility, which significantly outweigh some risks related to security and technical problems that might arise. Brokers implement various technologies aimed to ensure customers' protection and privacy against internet threats and frauds.

You access your account entering a user name and a password and you may be requested to change your password periodically. The advice is that you implement a password that is difficult to guess, using a combination of numbers, letters (both upper case and lower case), and special characters. You should change your password regularly and use a different password for each of your accounts.

Some brokers' websites also require a security certificate installed in your computer to access the account. Sometimes, you can have the ability to manage more than one user name and assign each user a set of functions and the ability to manage a set of sub-accounts. In this way, you might give to one user the ability to trade and to another the ability to look at statements.

Of course, you have to adequately protect your user name and password. The issue of identity theft has been in the news lately. When you download a program or file from an unknown source, you risk loading malicious software programs onto your computer. These software programs attack computers of online users and can monitor your online activity sending your information to the thief. Sometimes, these programs can log your key strokes, obtaining username and password information. "Phishing" is another form of theft and is related to the use of fraudulent emails and websites to trick you into revealing personal information. The must is that you do not respond to E-mails requesting personal information.

You'll need to protect yourself against identity thieves, such as hackers or phishers, when you use your online brokerage account. The computer should be constantly protected by an updated security software package (with anti-virus, anti-spam, and spyware-detection features) and a firewall. **Access to the commercial internet provides great benefits to users, but there are precautions that are mandatory to limit as much as possible, particularly when your broking/banking account is at risk.**

The best protection is using your own and dedicated computer or network of computers only to trade online. To surf the internet, which could bring you in contact with malicious software such as Trojans, you should use different hardware. When you use another computer, make sure to delete the Temporary Internet Files and clear your History after you log off the account.

Access your online brokerage account only on a secure web page using encryption. By doing so, the information exchanged with your broker through its website cannot be read by anyone else. You will notice a key or closed padlock in the status bar if you use Internet Explorer and the address of the website begins with "https://" when the encryption is activated.

Finally, log out completely when you terminate your online session. Closing or minimizing your browser or typing in a new web address may not prevent hackers from gaining access to your account information.

At the SEC website, you can read an interesting article about the issue of protecting the access to your online account. Online identity theft, unfortunately, is quite common and it is necessary to approach the inevitable advantages brought by technology innovations with the awareness of the associated risks. Being superficial on this issue could be very expensive.

Online Brokerage Accounts: What You Can Do to Safeguard Your Money and Your Personal Information

www.sec.gov/investor/pubs/onlinebrokerage.htm

Once you have logged in, you can find information about your online account and send orders to the markets to which you have subscribed.

Normally, when trading futures, you can see:

- Real-time Cash Balance, Account Equity, Purchasing Power, Trade Equity

- Initial Margin, Maintenance Margin

- Open positions, orders, average price

Trading equities or options, you can access the following information:

- Account Net Worth, Liquidation Value of Options, Marginable Equities Buying Power

- Option Buying Power, Cost Of Positions, Unrealized P/L, Realized P/L, etc.

Online you can access your account management functions, such as the ability to enter instructions for a check, wire, or Electronic Funds Transfer or see the funds status. Report management functions will allow you, for example, to view/print/download daily, monthly, and yearly statements.

Your online account information is updated in real-time, tick-by-tick. The brokers will provide you with instant access to real-time trading account information, including:

- open

- filled

- cancelled

- parked orders

- account and fund status

- real-time net profit/loss

- buying power and margin data

Most firms offer alternatives to online access for placing trades. Touch-tone telephone, fax, or simply the phone are the typical alternatives. You have to know how to contact these services quickly should you have the need to close a trade and your computer is down or the line does not work. Using the various alternatives might be more expensive; check with your broker the costs associated. Also take into account the possibility of delay by placing your trades, as your access to the market might be slower.

Sometimes, technical problems could impact on your capability to manage orders and positions adequately. Your modem or your computer might have a failure or the Internet Service Provider might have issues and not be able to provide you with the expected quality of service. Also, your broker-dealer might have issues related to its system or Service Provider. You have to be aware of the potential issues, because a delay in the access or a failure would prevent you from trading with the expected speed of execution and you might incur unexpected losses. Serious traders may want to implement different connectivity means to reach the broker's servers and have more than one computer networked. Brokers, on their side, have redundant hardware and software configurations to manage their business and reduce the risks.

If problems occur, you can contact a customer-service representative. Keep records to substantiate any problems and, if necessary, you can file a complaint.

An important point is that from home you can use platforms very close, if not identical, to those used by professionals. You can access a number of markets making use of the most sophisticated software analysis available. You can basically almost do for free what 10 years ago could have cost thousands of dollars.

Technology innovations and competition have opened great possibilities to the average investor or trader. However, although you may have access to real time quotes, the speed of your access to markets can vary a lot. In the era of algorithmic trading, where computers take care of managing complex investment strategies, a fast access to markets is very important, especially if you want to apply scalping techniques.

Margin

In a cash account, the customer is required to pay the securities purchased using the money in the account. In this case, the credit balance is the amount of money that remains after purchases. When trading equity securities, a margin account is a type of account that brokerages offer to allow traders to borrow cash to buy securities.

A trader might be required to pay, for example, only 50% of the value of a purchase and borrow the rest, using the securities as collateral. In this case, you could purchase a greater number of shares than you could have been able to purchase with your own funds.

Through the use of margin you increase your buying power, but you are charged interest. Margin loans can be highly profitable for brokerage firms. Purchases of securities "on margin" have grown dramatically recently. The amount of debt taken on to buy securities reached a record high of **$321.2 billion** in February 2007, according to FINRA.

Many investors and traders may underestimate the risks of trading on margin. Your brokerage firm has to provide you with a margin disclosure statement, where the risks of margin trading are explained: (www.finra.org/web/groups/inv_info/documents/investor_information/p005 895.pdf).

The risks can be summarized as follows:

- Your firm can force the sale of securities in your accounts to meet a margin call.

- Your firm can sell your securities without contacting you.

- You are not entitled to choose which securities or other assets in your accounts are sold.

- Your firm can increase its "house" maintenance requirements at any time and is not required to provide you with advance notice.

- You are not entitled to an extension of time on a margin call.

- You can lose more money than you deposit in a margin account.

The Federal Reserve Board and many Self Regulatory Organizations (SROs) have rules that govern margin trading. Brokerage firms can establish their own requirements as long as they are at least as restrictive (house requirements).

A **minimum margin** is required before trading, where, for example, you would deposit with your broker a minimum of $2,000 or 100% of the purchase price, whichever is less. Some firms may require you to deposit more than $2,000.

The **initial margin** is the percentage of the purchase price of securities that can be purchased on margin. It represents the initial payment (cash or marginable securities) required for a margin transaction. According to Regulation T of the Federal Reserve Board, the initial margin for equity securities is 50%. Some firms require a deposit of more than 50% of the purchase price. Be aware that not all securities can be purchased on margin.

The **maintenance margin** is the minimum amount of equity in your margin account required after you buy stock on margin. The rules require you to have at least 25% of the total market value of the securities in your margin account at all times. Many brokerage firms have higher maintenance requirements.

For example, for low-priced stocks (below $3-$5) both the initial margin and the maintenance margin might be higher or fixed at 100% .

If the value of the purchased equities drops below the maintenance margin, your broker may issue a margin call, which will require you to deposit cash or securities into your account. In case you are unable to meet the margin call, your firm will sell the securities in your account to bring the account's equity back up to the required level.

Be aware that your brokerage firm can sell your securities without contacting you and that you are not entitled to an extension of time on a margin call.

In summary, the use of margin enables you to leverage an investment since you put up only a portion of the purchase price and borrow the remainder, but it increases the potential for higher losses. The leverage it provides means that both your gains and losses are amplified.

You have to carefully understand the implications of using margin and decide if it is suitable for your investment style and your risk tolerance. Because margin exposes traders to risk, it's not advisable for beginners.

For example, if you deposit $10,000 in your margin account and put up 50% of the purchase price, you can buy $20,000 worth of securities. If you do it and the market value drops to $18,000, only 10% lower, your account would suffer a loss of $2,000 to the amount of $8,000, which is 20% of your initial balance (you are left with $18,000-$10,000 = $8,000). As you can see, the risk of leveraging is high.

At the same time, leveraging has a positive side. If the purchased securities market value increases 10% to $22,000, on your account you would make $2,000, which is 20% of profit. That's a 20% return on your cash although the stock went up 10%.

You can find detailed information about trading on margin on the SEC and FINRA websites:

Margin: Borrowing Money To Pay for Stocks

www.sec.gov/investor/pubs/margin.htm

Investing with Borrowed Funds: No "Margin" for Error

www.finra.org/InvestorInformation/InvestorAlerts/MarginandBorrowing/InvestingwithBorrowedFundsNoMarginforError/index.htm

You can read the Federal Reserve Board's Regulation T

Title 12 – Banks and Banking

CHAPTER II—FEDERAL RESERVE SYSTEM
PART 220 – CREDIT BY BROKERS AND DEALERS (REGULATION T) at:

www.access.gpo.gov/nara/cfr/waisidx_99/12cfr220_99.html

The Regulation T sets margin requirements at:

http://frwebgate.access.gpo.gov/cgi-bin/get-cfr.cgi?TITLE=12&PART=220&SECTION=12&YEAR=1999&TYPE=TEXT

When you enter into a futures or option contract through an individual account, you are required to make a payment referred to as a "margin payment" or "performance bond." I have described margin requirements in Part I – Products – Futures.

Trading commodity futures and option contracts is highly leveraged and small changes in price can result in large gains or losses in a short period of time. Beginners should be particularly aware of the risks when trading these instruments.

Each day, your broker will calculate the current value of futures and option contracts held in your account. If the equity in your account has declined in value to the "maintenance margin level" (about 75% of the amount of the initial margin), you are required to provide money to restore the initial margin level (margin call).

Statements, balance

Statements are normally generated on a daily, monthly, or sometimes even yearly basis. Most of the time, but I wouldn't dare to say always, they are available online, but they can usually be sent via e-mail.

The daily statement covers the trading activity that occurred during trading hours. Products can also have different closing hours when they trade at the same exchange. In any case, the statement is generally available a short time after the end of the trading session. Monthly statements are provided a few business days after the close of a month.

Normally, individual traders receive one statement for each account they have with their broker. Statements provide the owner of an account with the information about the trades taken, the balance (net of debits and credits for an account at the end of a reporting period), the profit/loss summary, the open positions, etc.

Each brokerage firm's statement looks a little different, but all statements provide similar information.

For example, the information provided could be the following:

- **Account Information**. It summarizes the account number, account type (e.g. individual, partnership, etc.), account capabilities (i.e. cash or margin), trading permissions (stocks, options, etc.) and the base currency of the account (EUR, USD and so forth).

- **Equity**. This section shows the balances. You could have a securities account balance (stocks, options, fixed income, etc.), a commodities account balance, and others. There could also be a section for each currency.

Then you could be able to visualize and filter the profit summary according to different criteria. A section could show the changes in your cash balance, including commissions, deposits and/or withdrawals, dividends, fees (such as overnight maintenance fees for futures, telephone order, market data, trading platforms subscription, etc.), interest, net trades, cash, prior period balance and so forth.

- **Portfolio**. It would display the portfolio of open positions and their market value. Positions could be displayed in their currency and converted into the base. Some statements also report changes in value since time of purchase.

- **Transactions**. The details of the transactions could be displayed. The following table provides an example of what you could expect.

Stocks/CUSIP	Date/Time	Exchange	Qty	Price	Amount	Commission	P/L
Wal-Mart Stores (WMT)/ 931142103	05/02/07 10:20:37	NYSE	1000	47.92	$47,920	$15	$150

Futures	Date/Time	Exchange	Qty	Price	P/L	Commission
ESU06	05/02/07 20:40:00	GLOBEX 1	1	1498	$100	$4.90

Be aware that every broker organizes the statement information differently, although the basic information is the same. For example, find below a sample of a daily statement of a US broker related to an E-Mini S&P futures contract bought on 23 March, 2006, and brought overnight, therefore requiring a maintenance margin.

```
ACCOUNT NUMBER: XXX XXXXX
FIRM/SALESMAN: X XX
STATEMENT DATE: MAR 6, 2008

THE FOLLOWING TRADES HAVE BEEN MADE THIS DAY FOR YOUR ACCOUNT AND
RISK.

TRADE  SETTL  BUY  SELL  CONTRACT  DESCRIPTION  TRADE  PRICE  CC
DEBIT(DR)/CREDIT

-------------------------------------------------------------------

3/23/6              1      MAR 06 E-MINI S&P 500         1293.25        US

                           GLOBEX TRADE

                    1*

US 1.20DR                                           COMMISSION
US 1.14DR                                  EXCHANGE & CLEARING FEE
US .02DR                                              NFA FEE
US 2.36DR                                  TOTAL COMMISSION & FEES


* * * * * * * * * * * * * O P E N  P O S I T I O N S * * * * * * * * * * * * *


TRADE SETTL LONG SHORT CONTRACT DESCRIPTION PRICE  CC DEBIT(DR)/CREDIT

-------------------------------------------------------------------

3/23/6         1           MAR 06 E-MINI S&P 500        1293.25      US
152.50DR

                           GLOBEX TRADE

               1*                                      1290.20
152.50DR
```

	US$-SEGREGATED	CONVERTED TO USD
BEGINNING BALANCE	10,132.58	10,132.58
COMMISSION	1.20DR	1.20DR
EXCHANGE & CLEARING FEE	1.14DR	1.14DR
NFA FEE	.02DR	.02DR
TOTAL COMMISSIONS & FEES	2.36DR	2.36DR
NET PROFIT/LOSS FROM TRADES	2.36DR	2.36DR
ENDING BALANCE	10,130.22	10,130.22
OPEN TRADE EQUITY	152.50DR	152.50DR
TOTAL EQUITY	9,977.72	9,977.72
ACCOUNT VALUE AT MARKET	9,977.72	9,977.72
INITIAL MARGIN REQUIREMENT	3,938.00	3,938.00
MAINTENANCE MARGIN REQUIREMENT	3,150.00	3,150.00
EXCESS EQUITY	6,039.72	6,039.72

In this case, the contract has been held bringing overnight a potential loss of $152.50. The maintenance margin of $3,150 left $6,039.72 as equity available to open other positions.

Total commissions paid were $2.36, taking into account broker commission, exchange & clearing fee, and NFA fee. It is not expensive compared with fees and commissions that we happen to find trading European markets or, when trading U.S. markets, opening accounts with European-based brokers. Globalization, however, advances and to be competitive, commissions by European brokers to operate on U.S. markets are under pressure. It is easy for a European to open an account in the U.S. and competition is very high.

The statement has to be checked carefully to verify that all trades executed are reported correctly. Report any inconsistency to your broker and ask your broker to explain details that you do not understand. The statement report only changes related to the reporting period and it is a very useful tool for a trader.

You can read the following North American Securities Administrators Association (NASAA) brochure, which provides useful tips and information:

Understanding Your Brokerage Account Statements

www.nasaa.org/content/Files/BrokerStatements.pdf.

However, using statements will not allow you to track and analyze the performance of your portfolio and the strategies you have applied. To do that you need specific software tools, which are available on the market. You can often find on the internet for free web-based portfolio tracking applications that provide some services.

Examples of free online tools are:

Morningstar portfolio management tools

www.morningstar.com/Cover/Tools.html?pgid=hetabtools

MSN Money Investment Toolbox

http://moneycentral.msn.com/investor/controls/setup.aspx?Redir=True&targ et=http%3a%2f%2fmoneycentral%2emsn%2ecom%2fscripts%2fwebquote %2edll%3fipage%3dpmx

Smartmoney.com portfolio tracker

www.smartmoney.com/login/?referID=1

Forbes portfolio tracker

http://members.forbes.com/membership/?gotoURL=http://www.forbes.com/
portfolio/index.jhtml&gotoDescription=Start%20using%20Portfolio%20Tra
cker&gotoURL2=/portfolio/about_portfolio.jhtml&gotoDescription2=Learn
%20About%20Portfolio%20Tracker&comingFrom=portfolio

CNNMoney.com Portfolio Management

http://audience.cnn.com/services/money/memberservices/member_auth.jsp?
source=money&pid=money.portfolio&url=%2Fservices%2Fmoney%2Fport
folio%2FMSPortfolio%3FreturnUrl%3Dhttp%253A%252F%252Fbcportfol
io.money.cnn.com%252Fcustom%252Fcnnmoney2%252F1%252Fportfolio
%252Fview.asp.

Bloomberg Portfolio Tracker

www.bloomberg.com/invest/portfolio/index.html

Risks: trading risks, broker default, currency risk, fraud

Investment risks have to be evaluated carefully, taking into account your financial situation, your experience, your tolerance for risk and your investment objectives.

You can have:

- non-systematic risks, which are risks associated with investing and are known also as business risks. Common business risks include management risk (also called company risk), and credit risk (also called default risk).

- systematic risks (or market risk), which involve economic factors and are related to the securities price fluctuations due to changes in the market's fundamentals and specific events.

Types of market risks:

- **Interest Rate Risk**, with the risk of fluctuations in the value of securities due to changes in interest rates.

- **Inflation Risk**, with a potential negative impact on the value of investments.

- **Currency Risk**. Non U.S.-based traders have to particularly take into account the currency risk. For example, European traders have to consider the Euro vs. U.S. dollar exchange rate fluctuations to evaluate the performance in U.S. dollar denominated instruments. If the Euro improves its exchange rate with regards to the U.S. dollar, your investment will have a lower value. The opposite is true. If the Euro decreases its value vs. the U.S. dollar, your investment will have more value. Do not undervalue this aspect because it may influence your final results significantly. During the past three years, the EURUSD moved from 1.20 to 1.50, a 25% appreciation of the European currency. At the same time the Dow Jones Industrial Average moved up from 10,000 to 12,500 as of March 2008. The stock-market advance has been eroded by the dollar depreciation for the European investor. Nonetheless, in the future, the currency risk could also imply opportunities for non-U.S. investors if the dollar-based gains in value vs. the Euro, due to the appreciation of the U.S. currency.

- **Liquidity**

- **Socio-political**

- **Country**

For more details, read the FINRA article:

Market Risk: What You Don't Know Can Hurt You

www.finra.org/InvestorInformation/InvestorAlerts/TradingSecurities/Market RiskWhatYouDontKnowCanHurtYou/index.htm

Risk is exposure and uncertainty about the market value of a portfolio. When traders approach markets, they have to be aware that they can be exposed to losses because of market fluctuations. Based on their own "risk appetite", traders may apply different styles of investment focusing on the financial instruments that best suit their investment attitude. Also, the strategies applied and the time frame traded reflect the tendency of an individual to take risks. No matter how risky a position is, the important thing is that a trader be aware of what he/she is doing and what the consequences of holding that position might be.

A risk-averse investor may not want to day trade stock index futures contracts, options or single stock futures. You would rather trade a cash account instead of a margin account. And/or you could choose a category of low volatility assets to trade. Awareness is the key point. Unfortunately, not everybody is fully aware of how nasty the market can be when it turns against you. Investors may not be fully knowledgeable of the mechanics and structure of the markets and instruments they trade. Often, they get enthusiastic because they see a favourable market phase and they take high risks – higher than what they can tolerate. Invariably, they get punished sooner or later.

Most investment losses are the result of market forces and factors, which have nothing to do with fraud. In addition to market risk, you have to be aware that there is also a risk of fraud in the investment industry. From the beginning of your investment process, you have to make sure you minimize the risk of fraud. In case such a situation arises, you have to know what to do and to whom you can file a complaint. You also have to know where you can find the right information, because you may be able to do something about it and recover at least part of your losses.

If you want to invest wisely, one of the first things to do is to avoid making investments based on information found from unqualified sources. For example, if the investment involves a small and/or thinly traded company, the risk is particularly high. If you are really willing to make such investment, you should check the financial statements from the company. The EDGAR database, which can be found at the SEC website, provides some useful information. Companies are required to file registration statements, periodic reports, and other forms electronically through EDGAR (www.sec.gov/investor/pubs/edgarguide.htm). "EDGAR, the Electronic Data Gathering, Analysis, and Retrieval system, performs automated collection, validation, indexing, acceptance, and forwarding of submissions by companies and others who are required by law to file forms with the U.S. Securities and Exchange Commission (SEC)."

Anyone can access and download these reports from the SEC's EDGAR database for free.

Be aware that all but the smallest public companies are required to file reports with the SEC – "including companies with 500 or more investors and $10 million or more in assets, companies that list their securities on a major national exchange (such as the New York Stock Exchange or the NASDAQ Stock Market), and companies whose securities are quoted on the OTC Bulletin Board."

The SEC (www.sec.gov/answers/infomatters.htm) provides some good general advice on information to check to make sure that your investment is safe from the risk of fraud.

Sometimes investors are attracted by companies who have filed for, or who are involved in, bankruptcy proceedings (Chapter 11 protection). The assumption is that the price may rise once the company emerges from bankruptcy. Be very prudent when buying these stocks as the risk is very high and may lead to financial loss. Although a company may emerge from bankruptcy, in most cases, as part of the reorganization, the existing equity shares will be cancelled. Normally, the creditors and the bondholders have a priority in the bankruptcy procedure to recover their investment, not the shareholders.

Be very skeptical about any investment opportunity that promises huge and guaranteed rewards. In the real world returns and risks are highly correlate; nothing is given for free. From a low risk investment you should expect typically a low return.

The SEC also warns about other typical internet scams (www.sec.gov/investor/pubs/cyberfraud.htm). **The Internet is an excellent tool to quickly and easily do your research about investment opportunities. Be aware, however, that it also an excellent vehicle for fraudsters.** Message boards, online newsletters, spam and chat are common ways for fraudsters to reach their targets.

We have already discussed how to choose a broker in the first paragraph of Part II. In summary, you can check your broker with the state securities regulator (see the NASAA at www.nasaa.org/home/index.cfm to verify their disciplinary history or with the NASD BrokerCheck site: (www.finra.org/InvestorInformation/InvestorProtection/p005882).

If you trade futures contracts, you can check with the National Futures Association (NFA) (www.nfa.futures.org), which records disciplinary actions against brokers. NFA's activities are overseen by the Commodity Futures Trading Commission (CFTC) (www.cftc.gov), the government agency responsible for regulating the U.S. futures industry. Firms must be a member of the NFA and be registered with the CFTC.

Brokers offer their customers protection for their account through the SIPC, which protects the equities accounts up to a certain amount of money. Should the broker become insolvent, SIPC would provide protection and coverage.

Of course, the protection does not cover the risk due to the normal price fluctuations.

The following are some resources that may help you find rules and regulations governing securities trading practices and learn more about securities fraud and your rights as an investor.

The **Securities and Exchange Commission** oversees the key players in the securities industry and regulates U.S. markets. The SEC works closely with other institutions, federal departments and agencies, the self-regulatory organizations and state regulators (www.sec.gov).

In the following article, posted at the SEC website, you will find the mission, the history and the organization of the SEC:

The Investor's Advocate: How the SEC Protects Investors, Maintains Market Integrity, and Facilitates Capital Formation

www.sec.gov/about/whatwedo.shtml

The SEC is organized into four divisions and 18 offices:

1. **The Division of Corporation Finance** "oversees corporate disclosure of important information to the investing public."

2. **The Division of Trading and Markets** "establishes and maintains standards for fair, orderly, and efficient markets." It regulates the main market players such as broker-dealer firms, SROs – e.g. stock exchanges, the FINRA, and clearing agencies – transfer agents (who keep record of stock and bond owners), and so forth. A SRO is "a member organization that creates and enforces rules for its members based on the federal securities laws". The Division also oversees the SIPC, which is "a private, non-profit corporation that insures the securities and cash in the customer accounts of member brokerage firms against the failure of those firms."

3. **The Division of Investment Management** oversees and regulates the investment management industry and "administers the securities laws affecting investment companies (including mutual funds) and investment advisers."

4. **The Division of Enforcement** "investigates possible violations of securities laws, recommends Commission action when appropriate, either in a federal court or before an administrative law judge, and negotiates settlements on behalf of the Commission."

The focus of SIPC is to intervene immediately to restore funds to investors with assets in the hands of a bankrupt brokerage in financial difficulties. SIPC is not meant to combat or provide insurance from fraud. SIPC helps investors not to lose their securities or money or wait for years to recover their assets.

At the SIPC website (www.sipc.org/index.cfm) you can find more details about the SIPC mission and the claim process.

Read also:

Answers to the 7 Most Asked Questions

www.sipc.org/who/sipc7questions.cfm

How SIPC protects you

www.sipc.org/pdf/SIPC_Booklet_Eng.pdf

Cash and securities (such as stocks and bonds) are eligible for protection. Commodity futures contracts, fixed annuity contracts, currency, and investment contracts (such as limited partnerships) not registered with the U.S. SEC under the Securities Act of 1933 are ineligible for protection.

SIPC funds can reach a ceiling of $500,000 per customer, including a maximum of $100,000 on claims for cash. Additional funds may be available after the cost of liquidating the brokerage firm is taken into account.

FINRA (www.finra.org/index.htm) was created in July 2007 through the consolidation of NASD and the member regulation, enforcement and arbitration functions of the NYSE. Virtually every firm doing business with the U.S. public is required to be a member of FINRA, which is dedicated to investor protection and market integrity.

It is responsible for registering industry participants, writing and enforcing rules, examining securities firms, enforcing the federal securities laws, administering a dispute resolution forum for investors and firms, and providing education to industry professionals and investors.

For more information see:

NASD Brochure

www.finra.org/web/groups/corp_comm/documents/home_page/p010668.pdf

Arbitration & Mediation

www.finra.org/ArbitrationMediation/index.htm

NASD Arbitration Awards Online

www.finra.org/ArbitrationMediation/ResourcesforParties/FINRAArbitration
AwardsOnline/index.htm

Rules & Regulation

www.finra.org/RulesRegulation/index.htm

Code of Arbitration Procedure

www.finra.org/ArbitrationMediation/Arbitration/CodeofArbitrationProcedur
e/index.htm

The **National Futures Association (NFA)** (www.nfa.futures.org) is the industry-wide SRO for the U.S. futures industry, that safeguards market integrity, protects investors and helps members meet their regulatory responsibilities.

Membership in the NFA is mandatory for everyone conducting business with the public on the U.S. futures exchanges – currently more than 4,200 firms and 55,000 associates. The NFA is an independent regulatory organization. It is financed by members and through fees paid by users of the futures markets.

The NFA makes available online the Background Affiliation Status Information Center (BASIC) (www.nfa.futures.org/basicnet) database. BASIC can be accessed for free. It contains registration information concerning CFTC registrants and it provides information concerning disciplinary actions taken by the NFA, the CFTC and all U.S. futures exchanges.

The Commodity Futures Trading Commission is a federal regulatory agency with jurisdiction over futures trading established in 1974. The CFTC provides government oversight for the futures industry. Each U.S. futures exchange operates as an SRO and governs floor brokers, traders and member firms. The NFA regulates every firm or individual who conducts futures trading business with the public.

The mission of the CFTC (www.cftc.gov) is to "protect market users and the public from fraud, manipulation, and abusive practices related to the sale of commodity and financial futures and options, and to foster open, competitive, and financially sound futures and option markets."

The CFTC is a regulatory body that encourages competitiveness and efficiency of markets, ensures their integrity, protects market participants against manipulation, abusive trading practices, and fraud, and ensures the financial integrity of the clearing process.

The CFTC runs a comprehensive market surveillance program that monitors trading activity in U.S. futures markets on a daily basis in order to ward against price manipulation, market squeezes, and other abusive practices.

Futures exchanges essentially must obtain CFTC approval of any regulatory changes or for the introduction of new futures or options on futures contracts. The exchanges also must have trading rules, contract terms and disciplinary procedures approved by the CFTC.

Important Acts related the CTFC functions are:

The Commodity Futures Modernization Act of 2000

www.cftc.gov/files/ogc/ogchr5660.pdf

The Commodity Exchange Act

http://frwebgate.access.gpo.gov/cgi-bin/getdoc.cgi?dbname=browse_usc&docid=Cite:+7USC5

At the CFTC website you can find the list of the exchanges and clearing organizations authorized to operate, and the products authorized for trading on U.S. exchanges:

www.cftc.gov/cftc/cftcexchproducts.htm

For useful resources for customers and investors see:

www.cftc.gov/customerprotection/index.htm

The North American Securities Administrators Association (www.nasaa.org/home/index.cfm) was established in 1919. Its mission is to protect consumers who purchase securities or investment advice. NASAA is an association whose membership consists of 67 state, provincial, and territorial securities administrators in the 50 states, the District of Columbia, Puerto Rico, the U.S. Virgin Islands, Canada, and Mexico. NASAA jurisdiction extends to a variety of issuers and intermediaries who offer and sell securities to the public. NASAA members "license firms and their agents, investigate violations of state and provincial law, file enforcement actions when appropriate, and educate the public about investment fraud." The NASAA website reports that the estimation of securities fraud alone amounts to $40 billion per year. NASAA supports the enforcement efforts regarding multi-jurisdictional frauds by facilitating the sharing of information.

NASAA focuses its efforts in representing the interests of state and provincial securities regulators and works with the SEC, industry SRO such as the FINRA, and other international regulatory bodies.

The NASAA website provides a number of resources and links related to investor education (such as the Fraud Center, the Investor Bill of Rights, and Issues and Answers). Make sure you check it to increase your awareness of risks of investment fraud.

Other resources:

The **Securities Industry and Financial Markets Association (SIFMA)** was born of the merger between The Securities Industry Association and The Bond Market Association.

SIFMA is focused to ensuring the public's trust and confidence in the securities industry and financial markets, and promoting effective and efficient regulation (www.sifma.org).

The **Investor Protection Trust (IPT)** is a "non-profit organization devoted to investor education. The primary mission of IPT is to provide independent, objective information needed by consumers to make informed investment decisions." IPT is an independent source of non-commercial investor education materials (www.investorprotection.org).

Other interesting links are:

SEC Proposed Rules

www.sec.gov/rules/proposed.shtml

Public Company Accounting Oversight Board (PCAOB)

www.pcaobus.org/index.aspx

Releases Issued by the SEC on PCAOB Rule Proposals

www.sec.gov/rules/pcaob.shtml

U.S. House Committee on Financial Services

http://financialservices.house.gov

U.S. Senate Committee on Banking, Housing & Urban Affairs

http://banking.senate.gov

Investment Adviser Registration Depository (IARD)

This is a filing system related to Investment Adviser registration, regulatory review, and disclosure information of Investment Adviser firms. FINRA develops and operates IARD.

www.iard.com

Investment Adviser Association

www.investmentadviser.org

Investment Company Institute

www.ici.org

Financial Accounting Standards Board

www.fasb.org

The American Institute of Certified Financial Accountants

www.aicpa.org

Securities Class Action Clearinghouse

http://securities.stanford.edu

Public Investors Arbitration Bar Association (PIABA)

https://secure.piaba.org/piabaweb/html/index.php

Sarbanes-Oxley Act Forum

www.sarbanes-oxley-forum.com/

SEC Law.com

www.seclaw.com/Welcome.shtml

Securities regulation

Securities regulation makes an effort to take into account multiple interests with federal, state, and industry regulators involved in the process to co-operate and make the market more transparent and fair. Regulation of U.S. securities markets started a long time ago, back in 1911, when Kansas passed the first comprehensive securities law. Before 1929, there was a need for a comprehensive federal regulation, but the prevailing idea was that it could impact negatively on the stock markets and the economy. Although most states developed securities laws, they were different and not harmonized. It was only after the stock-market crash that legislators started to introduce federal securities laws. Based on these needs, the SEC was created in 1934 out of the stock-market crash and the Great Depression.

A very important reference is the following:

The Laws That Govern the Securities Industry

www.sec.gov/about/laws.shtml

A lot has been done in the past decades by the SEC and other main players to regulate markets, although it is difficult to go through the series of existing similar and sometimes overlapping regulations. This is particularly true for the average investor, who does not have the ability or the time to do it.

There are two concurrent securities regulatory regimes: one at the federal level and the other at the state level. Federal regulation of securities began with the Securities Act of 1933 and the Securities Exchange Act of 1934. These Acts, plus the Investment Company and the Investment Adviser Acts enacted in 1940, which were amended over the years, are still the core of the federal securities regulation.

The first important Act issued is the Securities Act of 1933. Registration of securities and prospectuses for public sale of securities were significant elements introduced. The Act requires companies to provide investors with the relevant financial information before issuing securities to the public. The intent is to prohibit deceit, misrepresentations, and other frauds. The Act also makes securities fraud connected with the offer or sale of securities a crime. A defrauded investor can sue to recover his assets under the 1933 Act.

The disclosure of information through the registration can help investors to decide whether to invest in a company's securities. Normally, securities sold in the U.S. must be registered. The information filed by companies provides an overview of the company's business. A description of the security to be offered for sale, information about the company's management, and financial statements certified by independent accountants are made available to investors. Some offerings can be exempted from the registration requirement; in particular, they are offerings of limited size, intrastate offerings, and securities of municipal, state, and federal governments.

The Act can be found at:

www.sec.gov/about/laws/sa33.pdf

See also:

http://en.wikipedia.org/wiki/Securities_Act_of_1933

www.busadm.mu.edu/aim/documents/Securities_Act_of_1933.pdf

The Securities Exchange Act of 1934 establishes the creation of the Securities and Exchange Commission with the mission "to protect investors, maintain fair, orderly, and efficient markets, and facilitate capital formation."

The Act regulates trading in existing securities on the secondary market, empowering the SEC with the authority to "register, regulate, and oversee brokerage firms, transfer agents, and clearing agencies as well as the nation's securities Self Regulatory Organizations (SROs)."

The Act also requires:

- Periodic reports from publicly traded companies

- Filings of proxy materials before shareholder meetings

- Disclosures by anyone making a tender offer

- Registration of SRO

- Prohibition on fraud, including illegal insider trading

The Act can be found at:

www.sec.gov/about/laws/sea34.pdf

See also:

http://en.wikipedia.org/wiki/Securities_Exchange_Act_of_1934

The Investment Company Act of 1940 regulates the organization of investment companies, such as mutual funds and UITs to minimize conflicts of interest that could emerge from their activities. It was believed that "the national public interest and the interest of investors are adversely affected" because of the lack of "adequate, accurate, and explicit information, fairly presented, concerning the character of such securities and the circumstances, policies, and financial responsibility of such companies and their management."

The Act requires the disclosure of information when the product is initially sold and, following that, periodically to provide investment objectives and the structure and operations of the fund. Companies have to provide information about their fee structure and performance results. The intent is to maintain investors' confidence in these companies, but also to protect investors through the disclosure of information.

The Act can be found at:

www.sec.gov/about/laws/ica40.pdf

See also:

http://en.wikipedia.org/wiki/Investment_Company_Act_of_1940

The focus of the Investment Advisers Act of 1940 is the registration for investment advisers. Among other things, the Act defines the following situations of national concern if:

- their "activity is performed using the mails, means and instrumentalities of interstate commerce."

- their "advice, counsel, publications, writings, analyses, and reports customarily relate to the purchase and sale of securities traded on national securities exchanges and in interstate over-the-counter markets."

- "the foregoing transactions occur in such volume as substantially to affect interstate commerce, national securities exchanges, and other securities markets, the national banking system and the national economy."

The Act was amended in 1996 and it requires the registration of investment advisers with assets under management of not less than $25,000,000 or that advise a registered investment company.

The National Securities Markets Improvement Act of 1996 intended to reduce duplication of regulatory effort among agencies. Federal regulation, initially, was aimed to fill in the regulatory gaps left by state regulation, leaving to each state the power to regulate securities. Duplication of regulation and the role of merit regulation at the state level, however, remained an issue.

The Act is available at:
www.mfainfo.org/images/PDF/PL290.104.pdf#search=%22National%20Sec urities%20Markets%20Improvement%20Act%20%22

On July 30, 2002, President Bush signed into law the Sarbanes-Oxley Act of 2002. In response to corporate scandals that emerged at the end of the stock-market bubble, the Act mandated new corporate governance and accounting requirements for public companies. The Enron bankruptcy in 2001 and the 2002 scandals of Tyco, Peregrine Systems, Global Crossing, and Worldcom threatened to undermine the investors' confidence in the U.S. financial system. The response by the government to protect investors was fast and determined, mandating reforms to enhance corporate responsibility, emphasizing sound internal controls, enhance financial reporting, and combat corporate and accounting fraud. It created the Public Company Accounting Oversight Board (www.pcaobus.org) to oversee the activities of the auditing profession.

The Act was controversial due to implementation costs. There's been much debate about how American regulation is affecting the U.S. exchanges, competitiveness, as more and more IPOs occur in other foreign exchanges (e.g. London).

The SEC has been under pressure lately to draft changes to the internal-control standards.

The Act is available at:

www.sec.gov/about/laws/soa2002.pdf

You can find links to the *Spotlight on Sarbanes-Oxley Rulemaking and Reports* at:

www.sec.gov/spotlight/sarbanes-oxley.htm

http://thecaq.aicpa.org/Resources/Sarbanes+Oxley/Summary+of+the+Provis ions+of+the+Sarbanes-Oxley+Act+of+2002.htm

http://en.wikipedia.org/wiki/Sarbanes-Oxley_Act

Every state has its own securities laws and rules, the Blue Sky Laws, while the SEC is the main enforcer of the nation's securities laws. The Blue Sky Laws are a complex set of regulations from many different jurisdictions. They regulate the offering and sale of securities to protect the public from fraud. To make things even more complex, the securities environment is characterized by SEC rules and regulations, as well as regulations from the NASD and the various exchanges.

For more information see:

Introduction to the Blue Sky Laws

www.seclaw.com/bluesky.htm

Securities Laws, Rules, Regulation and Information

www.seclaw.com/secrules.htm

The Uniform Securities Act in 1956 was created by the National Conference of Commissioners on Uniform State Laws with the aim to provide a standard for state securities law.

From 1956 through 2002, successive versions of the Uniform Securities Act were drafted to coordinate federal and state regulation.

The 2002 Uniform Act intended to give states regulatory and enforcement authority, minimizing duplication of resources and coordinating with the federal provisions for investor protection and interest. The Act focuses essentially on registration and filing for securities offerings, registration of securities professionals and enforcement.

An important resource is:

www.uniformsecuritiesact.org/usa/DesktopDefault.aspx?tabindex=0&tabid=1

The Act can be found at:

www.uniformsecuritiesact.org/usa/DesktopDefault.aspx?tabindex=2&tabid=48

In April 2005, the SEC voted to adopt Regulation NMS (National Market System), which contains four initiatives designed to change the regulatory structure of the U.S. equity markets.

The topics addressed are:

- **order protection**, related to the "principle of obtaining the best price for investors when such price is represented by automated quotations that are immediately accessible."

- **intermarket access**, "which promotes fair and non-discriminatory access to quotations displayed by NMS trading centers through a private linkage approach."

- **sub-penny pricing**, "which establishes a uniform quoting increment of no less than one penny for quotations in NMS stocks equal to or greater than $1.00 per share to promote greater price transparency and consistency."

"[A]mendments to the Market Data Rules and joint industry plans that allocate plan revenues to self-regulatory organizations (SROs) for their contributions to public price discovery and promote wider and more efficient distribution of market data." This aimed to strengthen the market data system, which provides real-time access to the best equity quotations and most recent trades. For each stock, quotations and trades coming from different trading centers are disseminated to the public in a consolidated data stream." The full Regulation NMS can be found at: www.sec.gov/rules/final/34-51808.pdf.

In addition, Regulation NMS updates the existing Exchange Act rules governing the national market system and consolidates them into a single regulation.

As a reference you can read:

Self-Regulatory Organization (SRO) Rulemaking and National Market System (NMS) Plans

www.sec.gov/rules/sro.shtml

The NMS promotes fair competition among individual, but linked markets, as part of one single system, based on the interaction among buyers, and sellers, orders in a particular stock. The NMS on one hand incorporates competition among individual markets and on the other hand fosters competition among individual orders, promoting more efficient trading services and pricing of individual stocks. Competition among orders helps reduce transaction costs by improving liquidity and depth.

With this regulation, the SEC has intended to avoid the development of:

- isolated markets that could fragment competition among buyers and sellers

- a centralized system that would lack the competition among individual markets

Competition in equity markets involves:

- traditional exchanges with active trading floors

- electronic markets

- market-making securities dealers, who commit capital to facilitate the execution of large orders

- regional exchanges

- automated matching systems, which allow investors to trade anonymously

Broker-dealers are required to be members of an SRO. SROs set standards, conduct examinations and enforce rules related to members. Most SROs also operate and regulate markets or clearing services.

The Securities Exchange Act of 1934, the Maloney Act of 1938, and the Exchange Act Amendments of 1975, are related to self-regulation.

Self-regulation has been pursued in the U.S. because the cost of regulating the securities industry at the federal level was viewed as prohibitive and inefficient. The complexity of the issues also pushed in this direction, with the idea that the self-regulatory system could provide a good compromise between federal and industry regulation.

SROs are any national securities or commodities exchange, registered securities association, or registered clearing agency.

SEC

For more information on this issue see:

17 CFR Part 240

Concept Release Concerning Self-Regulation

Proposed Rule

www.sec.gov/rules/concept/34-50700.pdf

In the past, some concerns have been raised about the efficiency and fairness of the SRO structure. Dispersed order flows across different markets pose the issue of comparable regulation by SROs and market supervision. The advent of for-profit, shareholder-owned SROs has introduced potential conflicts of interest. The multiple SRO system is expensive.

The NASD and the NYSE Group combined their regulatory operations, creating FINRA, a single private overseer for all stock-market activity in the U.S.

The new SRO, which began operations in 2007 allows the harmonization of the rules written by the two regulators with benefits for investors and brokerages.

Sources of information

Websites

Investors and traders can access the internet to search online, and browse and retrieve financial information. European traders can operate in the U.S. markets leveraging the same information available to U.S. traders in real time. The internet offers a huge amount of information. However, this can present a problem for the average investor of how to filter the impressive flow of information made available by companies and media. Moreover, it is quite difficult to assess the quality of the information found. When new information is available, it is normally factored into the price of an instrument. Sometimes, however, information is not widely known or understood; that is why investors want to find reliable and timely sources of information, be it technical or fundamental. There is a significant risk to the average individual of becoming overwhelmed and overflowed by a mountain of information of uncertain quality and timeliness. Information management becomes, therefore, an important issue. Breaking news plays a significant role as it is a driver of short-term moves, characterized sometimes by high volatility. Being aware of earning releases times and dates can help a trader either to profit from short-term moves or stay out of the market to reduce risk. Rumours, misinformation and spam can be found on the web. Message boards, blogs, websites, magazines, newsletters, and forums can, if an individual does not have a sound and tested methodology, induce mistakes.

The benefits of accessing the internet, however, far outweigh the disadvantages. A few years ago, the average individual had to take information from the newspaper or from a broker, often a day or more late. Today, the information is available almost in real time on the web, providing excellent investing and trading opportunities.

The web also supports the education of investors quite well. There are a number of institutional sites that provide excellent material. They are very useful as they provide a great insight into the market regulation aspects and guide investors into the complex world of financial markets. The websites of the SEC (www.sec.gov), FINRA (www.finra.org/index.htm), and many others mentioned in the previous parts of this book provide an excellent and reliable source of information and education. Check the exchanges, websites to see what they make available to investors. Often, they represent an excellent source of knowledge of products, market structure, and data. Other websites, such as *Investopedia* (www.investopedia.com) and *Wikipedia* (http://en.wikipedia.org/wiki/Main_Page) provide investors with a lot of useful information and links.

A relatively new resource available on the web are the hundreds of thousands of blogs about finance. You can track them and search them through Technorati (http://technorati.com) and their number continues to grow. Bloggers elaborate information and market events almost in real time, and provide valuable information to those who follow the markets. They cover almost every aspect of investing and trading and present different trading styles and techniques, or in-depth analysis of economic/investing issues. The blogging phenomenon has really exploded in the past years and it is getting more and more popular. The number of blogs is so high, that finding the best blogs available on the blogosphere is not easy, especially for beginners.

More and more individuals, companies, and communities have considered starting a blog. You can find the blog of a private trader who publishes his/her own trading diary, the blog of a newspaper, or the blog of a respected university professor. You can have personal trading journals, technical analysis, fundamental analysis, options, forex, commodities, research, global/macro, trading, aggregator blogs, and more.

Selecting the blogs that suit your information needs is important. Also, the quality of the information you can find is fundamental. Good blogs are updated frequently, preferably several times a day. Their content provides an original market perspective, be it fundamental analysis, global/macroeconomics or technical analysis. Readers need information based on research, personal experience in financial markets, and sound market or economics assessments. Readers need to find a way to filter and select the enormous amount of information available. Blogs tend to be integrated in bloggers' communities, linking the information to broader contents posted on the blogosphere or the web. Readers search blogs that match their information needs and their trading style, looking for both education and entertainment. Bloggers tend to share their trading experience with readers, who contribute to the blog's growth and content evolution. Bloggers receive comments from readers, providing useful feedback and stimulating the exchange of views. The most successful blogs are those that have their content built by readers. The contribution and perspective provided by each individual, with unique points of view and knowledge, enriches the content of the blog.

It is not easy for a part-time blogger to gain new readers and to keep visitors returning to the blog. It requires a lot of work and commitment to provide fresh content based on readers' needs. Yet this is no guarantee that the blog will be successful. Good blogs provide valuable insight into investing and/or trading methodologies, indicate the process of moving from data to actions, and apply specific mental and technical models. Others provide an assessment on the general condition of the economy or focus on the psychological aspects of trading.

The successful financial blogs provide more information and insight than anyone can expect from a free service:

- a great number of links

- market updates

- articles

- in-depth economic analysis

These blogs, like any good businesses, provide value with consistency and build readers – loyalty. Blogs provide a service to readers; understanding readers – needs is the basis for success.

Daily Speculations (www.dailyspeculations.com/wordpress), by Victor Niederhoffer and Laurel Kenner, is by far in my opinion the best blog you can find on the web. Victor Niederhoffer was famous in the 90's because his firm, Niederhoffer Investments, printed excellent returns since inception, and in 1996 he was ranked as the number one hedge fund manager in the world. Disaster occurred the following year because of speculation in Thailand. He managed, quite impressively, to climb up the stairs of success again and write the beautiful book *Education of a Speculator*. Laurel Kenner runs the *Daily Speculations* Web site with Victor and Steve Wisdom. She and Victor co-authored *Practical Speculation*. The mission of the website is spelled out in its sub-title: "Dedicated to value creation, ballyhoo deflation and applying the scientific method in finance."

The philosophy can be summarized as follows: "We are animated by a desire to apply systematic, tested reasoning to improve our understanding, not by appeals to authority or the transition of charts. We believe that perhaps the most important part of the scientific method is asking the right questions – rich questions that if properly validated or refuted give information of a fruitful nature."

The information you can find in their blog is so valuable that you cannot believe it is available for free on the web! It is a living book with continuous new paragraphs and chapters written, as it gets several updates each day. The strength of the site is that it is run by excellent professionals such as Victor and Laurel who have an invaluable in-depth knowledge of financial markets, and their culture varies in many fields. The charisma of Victor has managed to gather the interest of more than 150 contributors with very different backgrounds. The quantitative approach based on counting in an ever-changing cycle environment opens your eyes on many investing myths and pseudo-predictions. I personally learn something new every day from the site about not only investing and trading, but sports, psychology, travel, barbecue, books, statistics, engineering and physics, software and programming, chess and checkers, and surfing.

Another interesting blog is *TraderFeed* by Dr. Brett Steenbarger (www.traderfeed.blogspot.com). "Exploiting the edge from historical market patterns" is the mission of the blog. He is the author of the books *The Psychology of Trading* and *Enhancing Trader Performance*. The blog is based on using historical patterns in markets to find a trading edge, but what may be the most interesting feature is that it focuses in performance enhancement among traders. The psychological aspects of trading are discussed here in many excellent posts.

There are so many valuable blogs that it is quite difficult even to propose a selection. Moreover, sometimes the most popular blogs may not have the most valuable content. However, here are some of the blogs that I like:

The Wall Street Journal – Marketbeat

http://blogs.wsj.com/marketbeat

It has great content and summary of the trading day's news.

Mish's Global Economic Trend Analysis

http://globaleconomicanalysis.blogspot.com

It provides thoughts on the global economy, currencies and commodities.

Econbrowser

www.econbrowser.com

Abnormal Returns

http://abnormalreturns.com

It offers a variety of links to primary sources of information.

The Big Picture

http://bigpicture.typepad.com

It gives a macro perspective on the capital markets, economy, geopolitics and technology.

The Kirk Report

www.thekirkreport.com

It provides market analysis and a variety of links.

Seeking Alpha

http://seekingalpha.com

It offers market opinion and analysis.

www.bloggingstocks.com

It offers market news and commentary

The Slope of Hope

www.slopeofhope.com

This is a blog for chronic bears!

Stock message boards and chat rooms have been spreading at an increasing speed on the web during the past years. They are becoming an increasingly popular forum for investors to share information. Yahoo Finance, MSN Money, Google Finance, and so forth provide an environment where traders can exchange information and trading ideas on particular stocks in real time as the trading day develops. While personal ideas about companies are posted on message boards, you may find threads not really focused on the subject and sometimes even unfair exchange of views. The medium itself is interesting as message boards represent a revolution in the way information can be shared among investors and the idea of contributing readers is great for the success of any initiative on the web. And indeed, boards are successful, but once again, the issue is quality. Threads are not moderated and inputs are not coordinated. What can be very valuable in other fields, can in finance and trading produce not-so-nice results. Threads are organized by trading subject or single stock. Important questions to consider are, why does an individual decide to post a message about a company? Why would an investor publicly provide valuable information to other investors? Sometimes it is because he or she has a position on the stock and wants to support the stock, influencing other investors. If the stock is illiquid, this may also occur.

I am not sure about the benefits of posting on stock boards. Individuals who post there often have a strong bias. The key point, however, is that investors, and traders' psychology brings individuals to share their uncertainties and hopes about their positions on the web with others. That is why, quite often, the contributions found do not provide any added value. Instead, if you go to boards and chat rooms where the market is followed in real time by full-time traders, you can understand their logic and methodologies, get to know the platforms and products they use, and gain access to books or resources on the web where they get information and so forth. Often, chat rooms are used by professionals to share their views and tactics in real time with real subscribers of premium services.

The SEC, on their website (www.sec.gov/answers/msgbd.htm) focuses on online bulletin boards – of newsgroups, or web-based boards. The SEC warns that: "while some messages may be true, many turn out to be bogus or even scams. Fraudsters often pump up a company or pretend to reveal "inside" information about upcoming announcements, new products, or lucrative contracts."

The fact is, "you never know for certain who you are dealing with or whether they are credible because many bulletin boards allow users to hide their identity behind multiple aliases. People claiming to be unbiased observers who have carefully researched the company may actually be company insiders, large shareholders, or paid promoters. A single person can easily create the illusion of widespread interest in a small, thinly traded stock by posting a series of messages under various aliases."

The phenomenon is so big that it is impossible to ignore the signs and the indications that these developments on the web provide. Boards may be seen also as a way to monitor the investing public feelings. Boards and chat rooms are welcome, but for sure, before following any type of investment idea, you have to analyze for yourself the pros and cons of your choice.

Trading forums and communities may be quality environments for traders to exchange their views and experience, and find valuable education material and articles for discussion. For example, two of the most famous sites are www.trade2win.com with more than 60,000 registered members, and www.elitetrader.com where you can find many active and professional traders. On these sites you can find information about brokers reviewed by members, data feeds, films, magazines, software, and links to other valuable websites.

Magazines

Magazines have been the primary source of education and information for traders and investors for years. Editors perceive the web as a challenge for magazines to find interesting and valuable new content in order to continue and attract readers. Most of them actually have adapted their business model, exploiting new opportunities offered by the web. For example, they offer premium access to their database of articles, or have developed online stores. Others manage premium sites that provide technical analysis or other services to traders. Nowadays, magazines can be found as printed issues or are available even online. *Currency Trader* and *Options Trader*, for example, can be downloaded online in pdf format free of charge. This business model is based on advertising published on the online magazine. Quite interestingly, **during the past few years, new magazines have emerged offering printed and online subscriptions, and have contributed to making education and information much easier and accessible to the average trader**. Magazines normally offer quite specialized content to their readers. You can find pure technical analysis magazines such as *Technical Analysis of Stocks and Commodities*, or magazines dedicated to specific products such as currencies, options or futures. Others, like *Active Trader*, provide information about trading, from technology to strategies, reporting to readers the experience of well known traders. Very interesting is also the focus on trading systems in all of their aspects, such as testing data and characteristics.

In an era of global markets, it is difficult to identify magazines oriented only to the U.S. markets. Here, however, I have listed some of the most popular magazines.

Futures

www.futuresmag.com

Traders World

www.tradersworld.com

Traders Magazine

www.tradersmagazine.com

Active Trader

www.activetradermag.com

Stocks & Commodities

www.traders.com

Traders'

www.traders-mag.com

Currency Trader

www.currencytradermag.com

Futures & Options Trader

www.optionstradermag.com/

Futures Truth Magazine

www.futurestruth.com

Barrons

www.barronsmag.com

SFO Magazine

www.sfomag.com

News services

On the internet you can find excellent news services and most of them are provided free of charge. Most financial information sites provide market data, in-depth news, quotes, statistics and analytics on financial and commodities markets. Information comes from an array of sources such as exchanges, markets, research services and other contributors. The information available is so vast that managing and processing the financial content provided is not easy for the average investor. However, the issue of timely and reliable information is so important for investors, that particular attention should be given to searching and choosing the right news provider. Quality of the news and information are key elements. The news is full of propaganda and can easily deviate the individual from his/her trading and/or investing plan. The average individual will never be able to compete with big professional firms when trying to assess the impact on the worth of a company of a specific piece of news. Similarly, it is quite difficult to predict the impact on the economy by an interest rate move. However, evaluations can be made at macro level and news can help make qualitative assessments. The individual investor, in my opinion, should try to move away from the buzz of the latest news, which often leads the public into making the wrong decisions. He/she should instead focus on longer-term considerations to support their investments and/or approach the market using a quantitative methodology. In this way, they can be sure to apply a sound and tested methodology without being trapped by wrong qualitative assessments made, for instance, because of an interview of a fund manager or a company's CEO read on the internet.

Below you can find a list of some popular news services:

Forbes

www.forbes.com

CNN Money

www.cnnmoney.com

Yahoo Finance

http://biz.yahoo.com/apf

Barrons

http://online.barrons.com/public/main

Bloomberg

www.bloomberg.com

Business Wire

http://home.businesswire.com

Dow Jones

www.dowjones.com

Financial Times

www.ft.com/home/europe

Market Watch

www.marketwatch.com

MSN Money

http://moneycentral.msn.com/home.asp

PR Newswire

www.prnewswire.com

Reuters

http://today.reuters.com/business

SmartMoney.com

www.smartmoney.com

The Wall Street Journal

http://online.wsj.com/public/us

World News

www.wn.com

BusinessWeek

www.businessweek.com

GoogleFinance

http://finance.google.com/finance

TheStreet

www.thestreet.com

Investing websites do not offer just one service, such as news, but rather provide multiple services to keep the reader on the site as long as possible by satisfying his/her information requirements. For example, many websites provide a stock-screening feature.

Stock screening is the process of searching companies that meet certain criteria. The user introduces a metric or criterion to search the database of companies, choosing within a set of variables. A screening engine finds and displays the companies that satisfy the variables selected based on quantitative factors. Screening allows users to select variables such as capitalization, revenue, EBIT, margin, etc. The number and type of variables and the quality of the database content in terms of freshness and accuracy of data is quite important to determine a stock screener's effectiveness. To find good applications you will often be required to pay a fee. However, it is possible to find valuable tools for free.

Below you can see some popular free stock screeners:

GoogleFinance

http://finance.google.com

Yahoo Finance

http://screen.yahoo.com/stocks.html

MSN Money

http://moneycentral.msn.com/investor/finder/customstocksdl.asp

Stockcharts

http://stockcharts.com/def/servlet/SC.scan

Morningstar

http://screen.morningstar.com/StockSelector.html

SharpScreen

www.sharpscreen.com/sharpscreenlite/default.htm

Charts

A typical feature of an investing website is some type of charting application. There are so many websites that provide good quality charts, that it is impossible to mention them all. Most of the companies offer charting software and data services for a fee. When they are offered for free, intraday quotes are always delayed.

Popular websites that offer nice charts for free on the internet are:

Stockcharts.com

http://stockcharts.com

Bigcharts

http://bigcharts.marketwatch.com

Yahoo Finance Charts

http://finance.yahoo.com/charts

Quote.com

http://new.quote.com

A very good resource that provides free delayed quotes and also intraday charts of stock index futures, commodities and currencies is the website:

Tradingcharts.com

http://futures.tradingcharts.com/menu.html

You can find many companies that provide research services on individual stocks, but also on specific commodities or markets. You can read about analysts ratings, upgrades and downgrades, reports, earnings trends, market outlooks and so forth. Websites and companies who offer research provide some information for free, but of course their business is to sell premium products and subscriptions.

Data services

Exchanges have different ways to manage information on orders, quotes and trades. The information produced by markets on instrument prices, transactions, and orders has great value. Quality of access to this information can influence the trading performance. The form, the timeliness and the depth of the information presented impacts on a trader's transaction costs. Data sales contribute to exchanges' revenues. Exchanges based on electronic trading systems have data easily available and at a lower cost with respect to floor-based exchanges. Generally, markets set up information distribution systems to distribute the information collected about the market's activity to their members and the public. Markets sell information provided by market data systems to the various data vendors. The public can access real-time services or time-delayed services. Customers that subscribe to real-time data services have to pay a fee to the exchange that provides the data.

In the table below, for example, you can see the monthly exchange fees applied by *Tradestation* for real-time data to non-professional subscribers of the major exchanges. Customers can access streaming time, sales data and ticker tapes using push technology, or access the vendor's server to get information using the pull technology. Data vendors allow customers to format and present market information according to their requirements in designed and customized pages and windows. Different technologies are used to present data to the public, including Java. Generally, the user is provided with a set of tools to graphically elaborate the data available. Most of the time, the user can implement a number of common technical analysis indicators to conduct his or her analysis of the instrument of interest. Time-delayed services typically provide 5-, 10-, 15- and 20-minute delay data. Delayed data is generally provided for free by the exchanges and many websites (e.g. yahoo.com or quote.com). The delay may vary from 15 to 30 minutes according to the instrument and the exchange considered.

Consider also that to elaborate the data provided, you may use a software platform that provides you with the technical tools you may need to perform the analysis on the instruments. Whether you follow technical analysis strategies or artificial intelligence, or other statistical and quantitative methods, you need specific platforms able to manage and elaborate the data provided in their specific formats. In fact, data can be provided in ASCII formats or, more commonly, proprietary data formats that require specific applications capabilities to be used. The access and the utilization of the different formats available on the market is not always easy, posing issues of export of data and the need of conversion tools.

The analysis software packages can be either provided by brokers on a fee-basis and be integrated in the brokers' trading platforms, or can be purchased to be used as stand-alone tools. For an individual investor, it is quite common to use the platform provided by his/her broker. In this area, the trading platforms provided are getting more and more sophisticated, often offering users extensive programming and customizing capabilities and features. However, the more specific and specialized your requirements of analysis, the more likely it is that you need to get specifically designed applications. Access to historical databases of instruments is also a typical issue for traders. It is quite easy to find historical end-of-day data of U.S. stocks on the internet (e.g. Yahoo Finance or Google-Finance). However, the management of databases and their update is another area of business for vendors. In fact, these databases can have great value for traders, especially if they comprehend a great number of instruments, and many years of data their available. Brokers, generally, make available the access to a historical database of the assets, but the availability of data back in time can be limited to a few years. Also, the export of data to other formats/platforms/applications (e.g. Microsoft Excel) can be limited.

In addition, there are vendors that provide end-of-day data of stocks, futures and other instruments, together with good historical databases and update services at reasonable prices. The download of data and the update of the database can be performed by the user when required. Database services are available on the market and can be found on the internet. The issue is that end-of-day data can be useful only to traders who do not trade short-term strategies and do not have specific requirements in terms of intraday analysis.

As online trading is developing and day traders, scalpers, short-term traders, and the general public are becoming more and more active on the markets, the requirement to have more granular data available for analysis is growing. Intraday data (from 1-minute to 60-minute data) are needed nowadays by many traders. Tick-by-tick data can be very valuable, but normally the number of ticks made available is limited. Having access to this data is very important to analyze a market's characteristics and dynamics in order to find very short-term inefficiencies that could be profitable for traders. That is why access to this information can be very expensive. Access to microstructure data related also to the dynamics of the order books could open new areas of analysis and trading, but data is expensive and extremely difficult to find. The tendency, nowadays, is for brokers to provide online accessible databases more detailed and complete as a service. The individual investor, who only a few years ago could merely see quotes in the newspaper the next day or had to call his or her broker to know a quote, can now access real-time data and extensive historical databases, and have good speed of execution using professional-like trading platforms. The gap between professional traders and non-professional traders has been reducing a lot with time. However, not having full access to order books and the exchanges, market data still poses limitations to the possibilities of an individual to fight on an equal par with respect to professionals on the marketplace, especially in terms of analysis capabilities.

Exchange	Fee
Chicago Mercantile Exchange (CME)	$25 – $55
Chicago Board of Trade (CBOT)	$55 (Market depth)
New York Mercantile Exchange (NYMEX)	$25 (EmiNY) – $55
Commodity Exchange (COMEX)	$55
Kansas City Board of Trade (KCBOT)	$20
Minneapolis Grain Exchange (MGE)	$15
New York Board of Trade (NYBOT)	$55
New York Stock Exchange (NYSE)	$1
American Stock Exchange (AMEX)	$1
NASDAQ Level I	$1
NASDAQ Level II	$11
Arca ECN Book	$10
NASDAQ TotalView	$16
Options Price Reporting Authority (OPRA)	$3
Philadelphia Board of Trade Indices (PBOT)	$1
OneChicago	$1
Forex	Free

Tradestation: Monthly Exchange Fees for Real-Time Data for Nonprofessional Subscribers at 1, March, 2008.

PART III:

Trading

Your first trade in practice

Before logging into your account to enter your first order, you need to reflect on the attributes required in order to approach the endeavour of trading.

I refer to SKICOD as qualities to be considered when analyzing the approach to markets and assessing whether it is likely to ever succeed as an investor and a trader. The acronym stands for:

- Skill

- Commitment

- Discipline

The first element is skill. Detailed knowledge of the market structure and the related products is a fundamental requirement. Having an edge is also the basis. If you buy and hold, you do not need an edge. If you want to be active on the markets, not having an edge will eventually bring you to lose money (if you are lucky it will be later rather than sooner). An edge you have today may also disappear. A market inefficiency you identify could fade away with time, reducing margins. Continuous research is therefore necessary to keep you competitive in the markets.

The second requirement is commitment. Passion for trading is necessary if you want to obtain above-average results. Only with sacrifice and determination can you get the knowledge, the experience, and the hunger for results that is typical only of ultra-motivated and committed people. Time is an important component of commitment. Unfortunately, time is a scarce resource and part-time traders suffer from a lack of time. Family and work may absorb an enormous amount of energy and also some hobbies have to find their space. The rest has to be dedicated to trading with great sacrifice.

Discipline is the last but not least requirement. This is probably the most difficult part. Building proper procedures and implementing them consistently is a complex challenge. **One must also consider the psychological and behavioural aspects of trading. Being able to build a map of your decision-making processes, defining your trading decision tree, and sticking to it are the keys for success.**

Part-time traders face several difficulties when approaching the markets. Let's suppose that a trader has developed and tested a system, which has an edge on the markets. He/she has managed to find a niche of market inefficiency, which can be exploited by a small flexible trader in and out of the market very quickly. The problem is that a part-time trader goes to work in the morning, participates in meetings, and the boss calls him/her right when the setup is there to be traded.

When the system gives a buy/sell signal, he/she is not there to trade it. This lack of consistency is a major issue. For a European trader, markets in the U.S. open at 15:30 European time and close at 22:00. The European part-time trader goes home when U.S. markets are open and finds the family-life requirements. Often they are more demanding than those of the office work. For a U.S. trader it is even worse; the domestic markets are closed by the time he/she gets home.

Being consistent with the trading plan is very difficult, even for the most determined and focused part-time trader. At the end of the day, although the system works fine and the trader is very disciplined, there is no way to outperform the market simply because he/she is not there to trade the system. I do not want to discourage anyone, but you have to be aware of the difficulties you have to cope with on real markets. On the markets, there is room for everybody provided that you have an edge, but you have to develop a strategy that can fit with the amount of time you have available to dedicate to trading. **It is useless to study and develop an intraday set of strategies if you will never be there to trade them, unless you intend to outsource the execution.** Rather, you should develop a longer-term approach that does not require a continuous monitoring of the price screen.

Keeping a trading diary is very important to track your results and develop your library of lessons learned. The process of going back to review the trades from a technical and psychological perspective is key to understanding mistakes made, but also to leverage on positive aspects.

Before starting the trading day, you must do your homework, planning the trades and the setups that would trigger your buy and sell orders. Planning is quite important and makes things much easier when the moment arrives to execute the plan. Without planning, much is left to discretion and emotions, which can push you to act impulsively.

The first thing to check before placing a trade is whether the money you have in your account is enough to meet the margin requirements. Suppose you want buy stocks, some brokers might ask you for 50% as an initial requirement for placing a trade on margin. If you want to buy a futures contract, you have to check the initial margin requirement of the specific contract you want to trade. For example, suppose you want to buy an E-Mini S&P Index futures traded at CME, you might be asked for $3,938 as the initial margin and $3,150 as the maintenance margin. If you trade one contract, however, you may want to have at least $10,000 in your account to make sure that you are able to manage some losses without having a margin call.

Suppose you want to buy a single stock future, you might be asked for 20% of the market value as an initial and maintenance margin. Check the various markets, trading hours. Hours are set by individual exchanges and may change both for the regular session and the extended trading hours. In some cases (e.g. Globex), you can have almost 24 hours of open markets. Although this is a great trading opportunity, make sure you understand well the implications in terms of liquidity and bid/ask spreads.

Find the ticker symbol of the security you want to buy. The specifications and the calendar of the futures contract you want to trade have to be known because you might be close to the expiration date. In that case, you would want to buy the next period contract.

The next thing you have to know is the commission you are going to pay for your trade. Check the commission tables provided by your broker. Normally, when you buy stocks you are charged for every share you buy/sell. When you trade futures the commission for your order is calculated per side and per contract.

You also have to check which securities you can trade electronically on which markets to know what type of execution speed you should expect. **The type of orders that the exchange and the broker support will help you analyze the possibilities you have to purchase and sell the securities.**

Important tips:

- Market, limit, buy stop, sell stop, and stop limit orders are the most common type of orders, but you can also use more advanced orders.

- Make sure you fully understand how they work before you trade, because otherwise you might find out at your expense. It is quite common, as a novice, to enter the wrong order.

- Make sure you confirm an order sent and do not automate the execution of orders before you gain enough confidence in the order types and the platform you use.

- Decide your stop loss level in order to control your risk on each trade. Consider your experience and financial resources and know how much you can afford to lose.

The equity order duration is another aspect to take into consideration in order to know how long your order is going to remain active. Normally the duration supported includes Day, Day + (extended hours trading), Good'til Cancelled, Good'til Date, and so forth. You may cancel your order manually before the duration. Once you enter an order, if it is not executed within the duration of the order (expire), it will be automatically cancelled. For example, if you send a day order, it will be cancelled at the end of the trading session (16:00 ET), if it is not executed before that time. Your platform will normally update you in real time about any change to the order status. Typically, the status you may have is:

1. sending

2. sent

3. received

4. cancel sending

5. cancel sent

6. cancel received

7. your order is out of the market

8. filled

9. partial fill

10. expired

11. rejected

Confirmations for your trades will be sent by e-mail the day after the trade is placed together with the balance.

Your platform should normally present you the order book with the bid and ask matrix. This window displays also the number of shares/contracts traded at each level and often also the VWAP (Volume Weighted Average Price), which is a measure of the price at which the majority of a given day's trading in a given security took place. The VWAP is calculated by adding the dollars traded for the average price of the bar throughout the day and dividing by the total shares traded for the day. It is sometimes used by institutional traders who want to break up a given trade into multiple transactions and try to have an average price of a long trade lower than the VWAP.

The time and sales window displays the time and the number of contracts/shares traded in each transaction. It helps you get a feeling of the size of the lots traded and the speed at which transactions occur. You should try not to be hypnotized by this window, although it is needed to monitor the market price and when deciding at which level to enter your order.

A manager window displays the orders entered, the open positions, the average price, profit/loss, and the balance. Sometimes, it shows also the historical trades and the performance. A chart analysis window helps those who base their trades on technical analysis to visualize the price and the technical indicators required by the trader for the analysis.

Many software platforms allow traders to fully automate their strategies. Once a strategy is selected and activated, the platform through the broker executes the strategy buy and sell orders automatically without asking (if so required) for any confirmation by the user. While this is a powerful capability for experienced traders, novices should avoid using it until they are fully knowledgeable of the risks involved. They have to know how the automation works and, most of all, they must have a thoroughly tested system.

Orders and order properties

Orders are trade instructions. Traders give instructions to the brokers and exchanges that arrange their trades. When they issue an order, they explain how they want their trades to be executed. An order always specifies which instrument, how much, and whether to buy or sell. It may also include specific conditions that a trade must satisfy. It indicates the price that is going to be accepted by the trader and can specify for how long the order is valid, when the order can be executed, if it is fine to execute the order partially and so forth. **Efficient communication is important in fast markets. Brokers must understand exactly what the trader wants, otherwise costly errors may occur.** Standard orders are, therefore, used on the markets to decrease the possibility of misunderstandings when communicating. Traders must know the basic terminology to trade markets. Let's see the main type of orders:

Market orders: a market order is an instruction to trade at the best price currently available in the market. These orders do not guarantee a price, but they do guarantee the order's immediate execution. They usually fill quickly. Traders who want to be certain of the trade execution use market orders to demand liquidity. A small market order usually has little or no effect on prices, trading typically at the best ask/bid price, while large market orders may have a significant impact on prices, taking up all the shares available in the book until the complete execution of the trade. When traders move prices to fill their order they have market impact. The price impact depends on the liquidity that is available in the market at that moment. It is important to remember that the last-traded price is not necessarily the price at which the market order will be executed. In fast moving and volatile markets, the price at which you actually execute the trade can deviate from the last-traded price significantly.

Example:

Dealers are bidding MSFT $23.62 and offering it at $23.65. On the bid side you have 500 shares. On the ask side you have 1,500 shares. John submits a market order to buy 600 shares of MSFT. He manages to buy all 600 shares at $23.65.

Dealers are bidding ORCL $14.81 for the stock and offering it at $14.84. The bid side presents 100 shares. On the ask side you have 400 shares. Above that level you have an ask of 1,000 shares at $14.86. John submits a market order to buy 600 shares of MSFT. He manages to buy 400 shares at $15.85 and 200 shares at $14.86.

Limit orders: A limit order is an instruction to trade at the best price available, but only if it is not worse than the price specified by the trader. When you issue a buy order, the trade price must be at or below the price specified by the trader (e.g. the limit price). When you issue a sell order, the trade price must be at or above the limit price indicated by the trader. If a newly submitted limit order does not immediately find a counterpart, it will stand as an offer until another trader accepts to trade its limit price, the order expires, or the trader who submitted it cancels the order.

Standing orders are placed in a limit order book:

- Buy orders above or at the best offer are called "marketable"

- Buy orders between the best bid and the best offer are called "in the market"

- Buy orders at the best bid are called at the "market"

- Buy orders below the best bid are called "behind the market"

Similarly:

- Sell orders above the best offer are called "behind the market"

- Sell orders between the best bid and the best offer are called "in the market"

- Sell orders at the best offer are called "at the market"

- Sell orders below or at the best bid are called "marketable"

When using a limit order, the trader faces the risk that prices move away from the order and it will not be executed. There is a price you pay to make sure your trade is filled. You pay it sending a market order.

> **Example:**
>
> The E-Mini S&P futures contract has the best bid at 1480.25 and the best offer at 1280.50. Let's suppose a trader wants to trade a short-term pullback. Jane places a limit order to buy at 1479. If prices correct down to reach the trader's limit order level, his trade will be executed. Unfortunately, prices continue to trade with sustained momentum and never pull back. Either Jane raises the limit order price or she has to give up the trade. She can cancel the order and enter a new order at a higher price, chasing the market. Or, she can leave the order active until it expires at the end of the day if it is not filled.

Stop orders: a stop order stops an order from execution until the price reaches a stop price established by the trader. Traders use it when they want to buy only after the price goes up to a defined level (e.g. the stop price). Similarly, traders use stop orders when they want to sell only after the price falls to their stop price. You can attach a stop instruction to any type of order.

You can use it when you apply momentum-based trading techniques or you might use it to implement your stop loss when prices move against your position. It is important to note that the stop order does not ensure that your trade is filled at the stop price. If the market is fast, you may get bad fills. In fact, a stop instruction provides the activation of the order only when the security trades at or above/below the specified stop price. These orders can be destabilizing in particularly volatile conditions.

You can also apply a stop order to a limit order. The stop price indicates simply when the limit order becomes active.

> **Example:**
>
> John wants to buy 1 E-Mini S&P futures contract only if they go above 1523.50, but he does not want to pay more than 1523.50. He places a buy stop limit order at 1523.50.

Market-If-Touched: this order is a market order that is activated when prices reach some pre-determined price level. Traders use this order if they want to buy when prices fall to their touch level. Similarly, they use it if they want to sell when prices rise to their touch level. After activation, the order becomes a market order and it will be filled at the best available price. This order is rare and most traders use limit orders if they want to wait for prices to reach their desired level.

Peg: A peg order's price changes dynamically with the market until the specified duration is met, the order is filled, or the limit price entered is reached. When you enter a peg order, you choose the value with which the order has to float (e.g. the best bid).

> **Example:**
>
> AAPL is $120.10 bid and ask at $120.70. Jane intends to pay no more than $120.40, but she wants to try to get the lowest price possible. When she pegs the order to the best bid with a limit of $120.50, her order will display at $120.10. As the bid changes, her bid will move with it, with an upper limit of $120.50 or until filled. Of course, if the market is strongly trending in the short term, using this order may prevent Jane from having her order filled.

In January 2007, the NASDAQ introduced the Mid-Point Peg order, which allows the price of an order to be pegged to the mid-point of the National Best Bid and Offer (NBBO).

Validity and expiration instructions: Traders can specify when they want their orders to expire. These instructions are important for limit and stop orders. In fact, with these type of orders, traders are not sure that the orders will be filled. Therefore, they have to tell their brokers what to do with unfilled orders. Open orders are orders still to be executed. Day orders are valid for the trading day and expire automatically at the end of the session. Usually, this is the default setting when you issue an order and it is the most commonly used type of instruction. Good-till-cancel (GTC) orders are valid until the trader decides to cancel them. Good-until orders are valid until a specified date. Immediate-or-cancel (IOC) orders are valid only when they are presented to the market. The portion of the order not executed in case of a partial fill is cancelled. They can also be called fill-or-kill orders (FOK). Good-after orders are valid only after a specified date. Market-on-open orders can be filled by the broker at the beginning of the trading session. Market-on-close orders can be filled by the broker at the end of the trading session.

Quantity instructions: All-or-none (AON) instructions require brokers to execute orders all at once. Minimum-or-nothing require the execution of a minimum size specified by the trader.

Other instructions:

- OCA – Orders in a One-Cancels-All group of orders will be cancelled when one of the other orders executes.

- OCO – One-Cancels-Other: a stop order and a limit order on the same market are linked together. The execution of one of the two linked orders results in the cancellation of the other order.

> **Example:**
>
> John bought 100 AAPL at $120.00. John issues a sell limit order at $123.00. At the same time, he wants to have a stop loss in place should prices move against him; therefore, he enters a sell stop order at $118.00 on an OCO basis. In this way, when one of the two orders is filled, the other will be cancelled. In this case, the trade executed can provide a profit of 3 x $100 or a loss of 2 x $100.

It is important to note that different exchanges support different types of orders. Before deciding to trade a specific product on a specific exchange, you have to verify what possibilities are offered in terms of orders and instructions allowed. Also, brokers/dealers can allow the trader to enter particular instructions according to the level of service provided. Traders, before deciding how to trade markets, should study in detail the instructions available and the flexibility offered by markets and brokers/dealers.

I have described only some of the most common orders and instructions available on the markets. Far from being complete, my intent is to provide you with an overview. The advice is to look for specific indications from your broker and each exchange website. For example, the website www.nyse.com/productservices/nysearcaequities/1157018931913.html provides the types of orders supported by NYSE and their description.

Bid/Ask Spreads

Traders indicate their intention to buy or sell by making bids and offers. Bids and offers include the price and quantity information that the trader is willing to accept to make the transaction. These price levels are defined as bid and ask. The quantity object of the transaction is called size. The highest bid price is the best bid. Similarly, the best offer price is called the best ask. A market quotation reports the best bid and the best ask in a market, which is often defined as the BBO (Best Bid Offer). The difference between the best ask and the best bid is the bid/ask spread. Buyers and sellers, through their bids and offers, provide liquidity to the market, giving other traders opportunities to make a transaction. Liquidity of a market is very important for traders. A market is liquid when a trade can be concluded without significantly affecting price. This occurs when the bid/ask spread is small and there are many open orders available for traders. Limit orders provide liquidity to a market, because they give other traders the possibility to make a transaction. Market orders or stop orders take liquidity because they demand immediacy of the execution. **The spread is the price paid by traders to have immediacy. When the spread is small, immediacy is cheap. When the spread is wide, immediacy is expensive.** This fact should be carefully evaluated when applying a trading strategy. In fact, depending on your strategy's average net trade, the spread could significantly influence your performance, especially if you apply scalping or short-term trading strategies. Bid/ask spreads depend on several factors. Among them, volatility is an important cause for the spread to increase.

> **Example:**
>
> Let's see practically how the bid/ask spread could influence your trade price. For example, Jane wants to buy 100 shares of AAPL. The best bid by the NASDAQ dealer is $120.10 and the best ask is $120.30. If Jane wants to be sure to buy the shares in the shortest time, she issues a buy market order, paying $120.30 dollars for 100 shares ($12,030). If she is patient, she may issue a limit order at $120.10. If filled, she would pay $12,010 or 100 shares. In this case, the price for Jane to have immediate and certain execution is $20.

A concept underlying bid/ask is scarcity. As described in the previous paragraph, only a limited number of shares/contracts are available at any given price. If you want more shares/contracts and you issue a market order you will, in effect, buy all available securities at that tier and then eat into the next tier or even more depending on the size of your order.

The spread is not fixed, it varies continuously, compressing and expanding. It responds to changing market conditions and the balance of offer and demand. Most bid/ask movements are due to noise, although studies are conducted to see if they have predictive value. Scalpers try to profit from inefficient spreads to make quick profits. The size analysis of the bids and asks is important to traders. In principle, strong bids should reflect buying interest with many participants displaying a big size to buy. Similarly, weak bids show little interest of potential buyers. The opposite is true for strong and weak asks. Comparing the strength in terms of sizes of bids and asks sides could provide you with an idea of the strength of opposing bulls and bears. However, very often, the displayed shares do not reflect real intentions of potential buyers and sellers. They are displayed with an intent of deception. Several tactics of deception are possible. Stocks and future markets are especially subject to these actions. When volatility increases, you will see the spread increase on fewer sizes and the price move fast. Be aware of the risks involved when deciding to open a trade in these conditions.

Slippage

The slippage represents the difference between a trader's estimated transaction costs and the amount actually paid due to market conditions or poor execution by the broker. Slippage refers to a failure to meet expectation with regard to the execution of an order. It reflects how an order's fill price differs from the price level that was entered. For example, if a sell stop loss order was placed at 1465 in the E-Mini S&P future contract and the order was filled at 1464.75, one would have experienced 1 tick of slippage on the order.

A market order is an order to transact a pre-specified number of shares at market price, which will cause an immediate execution, but is subject to price impact. Therefore, if you use a market order, there is no slippage.

If you use a stop order, then when the market trades at your price, your stop becomes a market order and it gets filled at the current market price. You have slippage because you have a target price but you do not get it. Your stop price triggers the market order and the price you get depends on the liquidity of the market, the bid/ask spread, the size of the order and the market volatility. Slippage is common on stop orders.

The faster and more volatile the market, the bigger is the slippage. The more liquid the market, the smaller is the slippage. In some cases, it may even happen that you get a good fill below your stop price.

The only way to avoid slippage is through the use of limit orders. By doing that, you demand a specific price to the market. Of course, the drawback is that you might miss a good profit because your order does not find a counterpart for the transaction and prices run immediately in your desired direction. If you trade within a short-term time frame using limit orders, you have to expect not to be filled every time. Note that if this can be accepted when you open a position, not being filled on a limit order might really be a problem when you want to close your position. Close monitoring of the market action is then required to make the proper decision. If you want to make sure that you are out of a position when you want to be, you have to enter a market or a stop order and accept slippage as an extra cost to pay for the certainty of the execution.

Stop loss

A stop-loss order is an order placed with a broker to close a trade when prices reach a pre-specified level with the aim to limit a trader's loss on an open position. A stop order allows traders to establish the amount of money they are willing to put at stake as a maximum on a trade, representing a way to control risk. The stop loss has to be defined in a way that the risk-reward ratio of the trade is enough to support the risk of trade. Trading without a stop might be very dangerous and expensive. **A stop loss is an airbag protection, from both a literal and psychological perspective.** You start a trade already aware of what you might lose. Especially in a futures market, where the leverage is high, not using a stop loss might be very expensive. **You may be forgiven by the market several times, but eventually, not applying a stop will be very costly.**

For example, let's say you just purchased 1 E-Mini S&P futures contract at 1520 for a short-term trade. You enter a stop-loss order at 1515. If the futures contract price stock falls below 1515, your contract will be sold at the market price. When you entered the trade, you decided that for that trade you wanted to risk 5 points, or $250. The reward you expect from the trade should be at least 2-3 times the risk in the range of $500-$750. It is not easy to decide which level of stop loss you should use. If the stop is too small, you are likely to be stopped before the trade goes in your direction. If it is too big, the risk-reward ratio might be too low to justify the trade.

There are several different techniques to define a stop loss. You can use a volatility based stop, that varies according to the market volatility conditions ongoing during the trade. In this case, the stop level will be adapted dynamically as these conditions change. Much less sophisticated is a stop loss fixed level based on past data testing and experience. Many traders also place their stop loss at graphical support/resistance levels; in this case it might happen that prices move to trigger stops clustered at resistance/support levels, and then fall back.

What is quite interesting is applying a trailing stop. Suppose you have entered a long position on a futures contract and prices move in your direction right away. You can trail your stop up according to different logics. For example, it can be fixed as a percentage off the highs that are printed over time or it can be moved up as higher lows are developed.

There are other factors that may influence the decision of your stop-loss level, such as your psychological tolerance for risk and losses. This aspect also influences the type of strategy you may decide to trade, where less risk-tolerant traders may concentrate on very short-term trades with tight stop losses. The volatility and the liquidity of a market have to be taken into account when defining a stop loss because in volatile illiquid markets, tight stops would be hit more easily.

Stop-loss placement can heavily impact your overall trading performance. How and when to place a stop loss must be studied carefully. Tests conducted on mechanical trading systems show that tight stops decrease significantly the performance of a trading system. Larger stops make the system perform better, although they are more difficult to manage psychologically. Finding the right balance and compromise is quite difficult. However, you must make sure that when you start a trade you have your stop loss in place, especially when you trade futures. It limits your losses and helps you cope with the stress of the trade much easier as you know what the maximum loss will be.

Most of the trading platforms, either applications or web-based, have the feature of inserting the stop-loss level when you open a trade. Make sure you understand well how this works before using it in real trading. You might insert an order in a wrong way and it might result in a loss. Having the stop already inserted when you start the trade helps you to be disciplined and follow the plan, as it is the broker that activates the order when conditions are met. What you can also do is mentally keep track of your stop-loss level and, when it is the right time, place the order. I personally find this last option more difficult to execute as, psychologically, when it comes to accept a loss you tend to hope for prices to reverse and go in your direction. Tick after tick you end up finding your trade in a much worse position. Trading platforms can also help you establish a profit-taking order in accordance with specific rules you want to follow.

The trading day, characteristics of trading during opening, mid session, and close – Making the time difference work for you

Traders focus their activity on different time horizons. They can operate applying a scalping methodology that leaves them in the market for a few minutes, and often only a few seconds, day trading, swing trading on three-four days position, or investing on an intermediate or long-term time frame. Whatever your strategy, if you are to follow the market through its intraday oscillations to profit from them, you should be aware of the market characteristics during the different times of the day. You might find out that a technique you want to apply, because it suits your personal and psychological character, works better right after the open rather than at midday or late close to the end of session.

During the day, certain time frames usually offer more liquidity and trendy action. Other time frames present typically low liquidity and choppy price movement. Depending on your trading style, you will select the type of "market action" that you prefer. Also, the composition of the trading participants changes as the day progresses and influences the market's behaviour.

The morning volume often brings volatile moves during the first 30-60 minutes of trading. Often, the high or low of the day is printed near the open. Near the open and the close you normally have the highest volume of the trading session. The first morning action establishes a trading range that will be used by some traders as a reference for their trading strategies during the day. Open gaps provide immediate signposts for reversals and breakouts. Gap closures or failures and short-term key levels established during the morning action influence the rest of the day. At lunch-time you have the so called "dead zone." Less traders operate in the market as, at this time, most of them have already placed their positions for the day. This phase is usually characterized by low directionality and low volume. Normally, between 11:30 ET and 13:30 ET you have the lowest volume of the day. While public participation dominates the open, this part of the day belongs to professionals and institutions. After lunch and until the end of the session, the activity picks up again.

The last hour of trading is the "power hour." Large volume volatility provides good trading opportunities. When prices breakout from the day's trading range, traders fight their battle for the last directional move of the day or the fading of the breakout, with many players trapped on the wrong side of the market and adding fuel to the reversal. During the last hour you see big lots traded. It reflects the fact that at this time of the day, character is driven by big players. Intermarket relationships may have an influence at this time, because of the different time the various markets end their sessions. The final minutes of the session provide peaks in volume because of traders settling down their positions. Extended trading hours are getting increasingly important. However, they rarely impact on the general market direction. Most participants use these times to complete strategies initiated during the regular session. Some might consider exploiting the overnight market action. Others enter new positions when companies release news in the after market.

Morning	Midday	Afternoon
Directionality, Volume Public participation	Choppy Low volume Professionals	Directionality, Volume

European traders can benefit from the time difference between Europe and the U.S. The market opens at 15:30 European time. In the morning, U.S. markets can be traded mainly on the electronic contracts of the Globex, such as the E-Mini's or the American stocks listed on European markets. The Globex during the night hours is not particularly active, but it is liquid enough and follows to some extent the variations occurring in the Asian markets during the night and the European markets in the morning. Traders in Europe can continue to follow U.S. markets after the closure in Europe. The regular session in the U.S. ends at 22:00 European time for the stocks and at 22:15 European time for the futures on Globex. Especially if you are a part-time trader or scalper, at the end of your work day you can still find the time to trade during the last part of the trading day in the U.S. and the "power hour."

There is not only a daily cycle. You can also see different behaviours through weekly and monthly periods. There are many studies focused on the relationships and characteristics of the day of the week. Different days of the week can be influenced by economic reports. Options expire on a specific day and certain reports occur on a specific day of the month. Study the calendar of periodic reports release to know if you are to expect increased volatility on those days. Some traders do not trade when important numbers are released, others just await these days because the volatile environment fits their trading style.

Seasonal variations can also have an impact on the market:

- Pre- or post-holiday trading sessions are characterized by light volume and often deceptive moves.

- The end of each quarter triggers window dressing by mutual funds and institutions.

- Tax issues influence liquidity on the market in specific periods of the year.

- Summer months present less participation by the public.

- Commodities, by their nature, are exposed to seasonality more than other instruments.

Stock markets are said to follow seasonal cycles and there are popular beliefs about the market's behaviour at certain times of the year, such as the "sell in May and go away", the Santa Claus rally, the January effect, or in particular situations, such as the Presidential cycle. Before basing your trading decisions on these assumptions, accurate testing and counting should be executed.

Trading systems

Traders have to find a way to approach the markets that best suit their personality. **My opinion is that the methodology should be as mechanical as possible and should leave out emotions and attitude. The trading methodology has to be designed, tested, and applied in a scientific and mechanical way, leaving the human factor out of the game.** A tested approach has to be followed with discipline. Of course there are also intuitive traders, and many can be successful traders. The validity of their approach is not measurable, although their results in the long term are. For those who want to approach mechanical trading and trading systems, there are various degrees of automation that you can blend into the decision-making process of a trade. You can decide to only partially automate your trades. For example, you can let a system provide you with the set-up and trigger to open a trade and then you manage the trade discretionally, moving your stop and finally deciding on the exit point.

The extreme of this approach is to trade fully mechanically. Although this seems the ultimate frontier of the part-time trader, it is quite difficult for an individual to program a trading system able to adapt to the different market conditions and take into account the numerous variables that influence markets. It is also quite difficult to compete with professionals and institutions who run algorithmic execution systems. With this premise, it might prove difficult for an individual to be competitive against these big players using a discretionary approach. It seems that most of the individual traders are not profitable (some say up to 90%). The financial system sucks from them the energy and the money to be fed and sustained, continuously working to attract new losers. Competition for profits is very high and the game is expensive (commissions, taxes, connectivity, information and time are only some of the costs). The best approach for them would be to benefit from the long-term up drift of stocks and not be involved too much in the short-term overtrading in and out.

If you decide to enter the trading arena, you must do so being aware of the risks and approach the market with a sound and scientific methodology. **If you decide to trade systematically, you must verify whether the rules you have established to apply have any probability to work in real markets.** It often happens that traders want to follow some type of rules only after they have experienced losses. **Many misinterpret experiencing luck, even for a long time in case of prolonged bull markets, with their ability as traders.** In a bull market, mistakes are forgiven most of the time as, sooner or later, prices resume the original trend and allow a trade to break even. A novice and lucky trader should ask himself with humility: "What happens if the market conditions change? Would I still be able to navigate stormy waters with my methodology?"

Being aware of the consequences of trading can push you to start seriously developing a trading plan. Realizing you need a plan is already an important step. Deciding that you need a trading system to support your decision is the second important step.

When designing a trading system, you need rules to define the underlying trend (up or down), the setup and trigger conditions to generate buy and sell orders. You have to define a method of entry that also takes into account commissions and slippage. Risk management has to be defined as well as your money-management rules. Filters such as trend and volatility indicators may be used to enhance your system.

My opinion is that you cannot have a valid system for every type of asset and with an extremely long lifespan. In fact, the concept of ever-changing cycles, so well described by Victor Niederhoffer in his books, is such that markets continuously change their behaviour and characteristics dynamically. **You cannot find a system that works with any type of asset, and you cannot ask a system to be valid and perform forever.** The market structure and the characteristics of the different instrument traded in terms of participants, liquidity and so forth, makes it quite impossible to believe that you can develop a system that works at the same time on currencies, futures and stocks. You have to be flexible enough to understand when the underlying conditions that make your system profitable today are changing, setting the stage for reducing and removing your system's edge.

Back-testing is a practical way to test the strength of your beliefs and ideas about the market and remove subjectivity about them. Back-testing also allows you to monitor how your system reacts to drawdown. Use in-sample and out-of-sample data. There are many ways to conduct back testing and, if you are willing to be serious about it, my advice is to get into the details to learn the different types of methodologies.

You want to make sure that the system you develop is robust enough to the ever-changing cycle context and is not over optimized. My opinion on this issue is that the length of past data should not be defined as a fixed number. To run the tests, data selection should reflect criteria of behaviour observed in relationship with the scope of your test objectives. In the ever-changing cycle process, you might recognize that a cycle has changed because of increased volatility or directionality or something else you have identified as your guiding parameters of the market "personality." In this case, your length could vary a lot. For example, if you assume that a new paradigm began in 2003 with a low-volatility environment, and this is relevant for the assumptions that you want to demonstrate with your testing activity, than you could use a 600-day data test set.

Finally, if the system depends on a few very good trades, it is likely that in reality it will not work. Long negative streaks and large drawdown tend to cause system traders to stop trading their system. System development helps us prove to ourselves that methods we have identified work, rather than just randomly hope that they will work in the future.

On the market you can find many commercial trading systems. This is part of a huge business. Often these systems do not disclose their rules and work like black boxes. Traders can pay from a few hundred dollars to thousands of dollars for these systems, whose robustness and validity is difficult to be assessed. Be very careful and prudent when approaching this market. There are websites where you can find these systems tracked and rated and offered either for sale or subscribed monthly to get their trading signals.

For example, *Collective2* (www.collective2.com) is a website that monitors more than 3,000 trading systems. You can apply the trading systems of your choice to your own brokerage account. *Futures Truth Magazine* (www.futurestruth.com/index.htm) is dedicated to the world of publicly offered trading systems. The public is flooded with trading systems. Many traders have purchased systems only to find out later that the system is worthless. The purpose of *Futures Truth* is "to provide information to assist you in both the purchasing of and the actual decision to trade a system." They track 100% and test for a specified amount of months mechanical, publicly offered trading systems and then publish the results.

An option if you are a part-time trader and do not have the time to trade the system you have developed is to find a broker that trades the signal provided by your system. Of course, this service will be more expensive in terms of commissions with respect to the average commissions applied by brokers, but it can be a good solution if you do not have time to apply the trading strategy's signal yourself.

Many platforms enable users to design, historically test, and optimize their own custom trading strategies. Often they use proprietary technology, such as the **Tradestation EasyLanguage** (www.tradestation.com), which lets you describe and test your ideas against historical data using simple, English-like statements and trading terms. Another popular software is **Metastock**, which allows you to create, back-test, compare, and customize strategies providing detailed reports (www.equis.com). With these instruments, the individual trader with good programming skills can develop his/her own system, back-test it and trade it. The strategies developed can be very complex and sophisticated. On the market and in forums you can find add-ons and libraries of code to help you develop your strategies, software modules. It is impressive how in the past years the average trader has managed to access the technology at lower and lower costs. With everybody available to develop and apply the most sophisticated strategies, competition has moved to even more complex strategies based on algorithmic trading and high-speed connections.

Automated trading, program trading

The word algorithm originates from Arabic and can be defined as a procedure for solving a mathematical problem in a finite number of steps that frequently involves repetition of an operation.

The word is derived from Muhammad ibn Musa al-Khwarizmi, who was a mathematician and astronomer whose major works introduced Hindu-Arabic numerals and the concepts of algebra into European mathematics. See *Wikipedia* (http://en.wikipedia.org/wiki/Al-Khwarizmi) and *Encyclopaedia Britannica Online* at www.britannica.com/eb/article-9045366/al Khwarizmi to learn more about him. A Latinized version of his name created the term algorithm.

When applied to trading, algorithmic techniques are applications of mathematical calculations to electronic trading in order to efficiently execute buy or sell orders of a defined size. It is most commonly used by large investors, such as pension funds, mutual funds and hedge funds, which have to execute large orders striving to obtain the best possible price without significantly affecting the security's price.

These quantitative models divide large orders into small lots, which have a limited impact on market price, according to specific rules, and automatically generate trade instructions based on specific objectives and parameters. The procedure continues until the order is either filled or withdrawn.

Algorithmic trading may be used in any investment strategy, for example market-making, spreading, and arbitrage. See the *Wikipedia* website to learn more about algorithmic trading at:
http://en.wikipedia.org/wiki/Algorithmic_trading.

Large investors use this technology to manage their strategies, integrating their algorithm into the order-management system or execution-management system with the objective of improving the performance and speed of execution. Algorithmic trading can be applied to equity/options and futures exchanges by brokers, dealers, market makers, specialists, trading firms, scalpers, day traders, and quantitative traders.

Algorithms are growing at a fast pace and their implementation poses some serious questions about the ability of the exchanges to support the impressive flow of orders coming from investors using algorithm.

Program trading is defined as a wide range of portfolio trading strategies involving the purchase or sale of 15 or more stocks having a total market value of $1 million or more. For example, index arbitrage is defined as the purchase or sale of a basket of stocks in conjunction with the sale or purchase of a derivative product, such as index futures, in order to profit from the price difference between the basket and the derivative product. To give you an idea of the extension of this phenomenon, NYSE tracks the program trading statistics on a daily basis to assess the impact of program trading on the regular functioning of the market. The NYSE releases the program-trading data submitted by its member firms weekly. For example, from May 29 to June 2, 2007, program trading amounted to 37.4% of NYSE average daily volume of 3,347.7 million shares, or 1,252.2 million program shares traded a day. In all markets, program trading averaged 2,551.5 million shares a day.

Computers perform at increasing speed what traders used to do by hand. Based on real-time and historical data, algorithms identify trading opportunities and determine optimal timing. This type of technology can put electronic trading systems under pressure with high burst rates of orders per second.

The velocity and the growth of volume of trading stress the technology available at the exchanges in terms of latency and capacities, especially when firms rapidly delete and add orders. There has been a growth in the ratio of orders to fill. Order-book transactions per second continue to grow. In particular cases, the latency can increase. The open of markets in the morning is typically a moment when transaction volumes reach their peak for the day.

It is clear that algorithmic trading represents with its risks and opportunities the future of modern markets towards a more efficient functioning of the markets where competition and liquidity compress spreads and lower transaction costs. The continuous upgrade of the technology of the exchanges to meet the demanding requirements of investors will support this process.

Costs involved in the implementation of algorithmic trading are significant. Consider that as firms and traders need fast data they implement direct feeds, buying the data directly from the exchange. However, a firm needs to connect to multiple sites and you have seen in the first part of the book how complex the scenario is in the U.S. with many exchanges, ECNs, and products. Often exchanges and ECNs implement different types of data-feed formats and symbology, which have to be normalized and consolidated before they can be used.

Storage is also a significant issue, as stored data is used for back testing and its amount is impressive.

It is true that individual traders today can enter the world of automation. Several commercial platforms support the programmed execution of instructions. You have to carefully consider both the potential and the risks of a program automatically executing orders. Moreover, depending on the strategy, the fact that the individual trader may not have the same speed of execution, and access to markets of large institutions may represent a disadvantage. However, it is impressive how fast during the past 10 years individual traders have reduced the gap in terms of technology, real-time data, and costs to access the market with regards to professional firms. This process will continue in the years to come, creating more and more opportunities.

You can find a number of interesting articles about algorithmic trading at:

www.ftmandate.com/news/categoryfront.php/id/95/ALGORITHMIC_TRA DING.html

Appendices

Exchanges

New York Stock Exchange

✉ 11 Wall Street
New York, NY 10005
☎ +1 212 656 3000
💻 www.nyse.com

The NASDAQ Stock Market

✉ One Liberty Plaza
165 Broadway
New York, NY 10006
☎ +1 212 401 8700
💻 www.nasdaq.com

American Stock Exchange

✉ 86 Trinity Place
New York, NY 10006
☎ +1 212 306 1000
Information Help Desk
+1 866 422 AMEX (+1 866 422 2639)
💻 www.amex.com

Chicago Board of Trade

✉ 141 West Jackson Boulevard
Chicago, Illinois 60604-2994
☎ +1 312 435 3500
💻 www.cbot.com

Chicago Mercantile Exchange

✉ 20 South Wacker Drive
Chicago, Illinois 60606
☎ +1 312 930 1000
💻 www.cme.com

Kansas City Board of Trade

✉ 4800 Main Street, Suite 303
   Kansas City, MO 64112
☎ +1 816 753 7500
💻 www.kcbt.com

New York Mercantile Exchange

✉ World Financial Center
   1 North End Avenue
   New York, NY 10282-1101
☎ +1 212 299 2000
💻 www.nymex.com

Chicago Board of Options Exchange

✉ 400 South LaSalle Street
   Chicago, IL 60605
☎ +1 312 786 5600
   +1 312 786 5600
   +1 312 786 5600
💻 www.cboe.com

OneChicago

✉ 141 West Jackson Boulevard
   Suite 2240
   Chicago, IL 60604
☎ +1 312 424 8500
   Toll-free: +1 800 752 4100
💻 http://onechicago.com

Minneapolis Grain Exchange

✉ 400 South 4th Street
   Minneapolis, MN 55415
☎ +1 612 321 7101
   Toll-free: +1 800 827 4746
💻 www.mgex.com

International Securities Exchange Holdings, Inc.

✉ Corporate Headquarters
60 Broad Street
New York, NY 10004
☎ +1 212 943 2400
🖳 www.iseoptions.com
www.isestock.com

IntercontinentalExchange

✉ 2100 RiverEdge Parkway
Suite 500
Atlanta, Georgia 30328
☎ +1 770 857 4700
🖳 www.theice.com

The Chicago Stock Exchange

✉ 1 Financial Place
440 South LaSalle Street
Chicago, Illinois 60605
☎ +1 312 663 2222
🖳 www.chx.com

Boston Stock Exchange

✉ 100 Franklin Street
Boston, MA 02110
☎ +1 617 235 2000
🖳 www.bostonstock.com
www.bostonexchange.com
www.bostonoptions.com

Philadelphia Stock Exchange

✉ 1900 Market Street
Philadelphia, PA 19103
☎ +1 215 496 5000
+1 215 496 5000
🖳 www.phlx.com

National Stock Exchange

✉ 440 South LaSalle Street
Suite 2600
Chicago, IL 60605
☎ +1 312 786 8803
🖳 www.nsx.com

OTC Bulletin Board

☎ +1 301 978 8263
🖳 www.otcbb.com

Pink Sheets

✉ Pink Sheets LLC
304 Hudson Street 2nd Floor
New York, NY 10013
☎ +1 212 896 4400
🖳 www.pinksheets.com
www.otcqx.com

Brokers

In the following list, you can find brokers that can be of interest when considering trading securities in the U.S. Far from being a complete list, it provides you with the means to contact the firms and find detailed information about the services that they provide.

The list contains:

- Direct-Access Stock Brokerages, from whom active traders get lower costs for high-volume trades

- Direct-Access Futures Brokerages, who provide services to futures and option traders. They access the exchange order-matching engines (e.g. Globex) and in-the-pit systems that deliver orders to brokers on the floor.

- Stock Brokerages, which include both full-service and discount stock brokerages. For discount brokers the commission and fees and quality of execution are important. From full-service brokers you should expect competitiveness of investment research and investment and financial planning services.

- Futures Brokerages

- Currency Brokerages

As with the other following lists about data and software providers, this does not intend to be a complete and exhaustive list of firms available on the markets and the services offered. Neither does it intend to assume that the brokers listed are the best available, but rather it should be used as an initial guide to research the fast-changing world of brokerages.

Charles Schwab Active Trader

✉   Charles Schwab & Co. Inc.
   Attn: Global Operations
   PO Box 2912
   Phoenix, AZ 85062-2912
   ☎ +1 888 245 6824
💻   www.schwabat.com
   www.schwab.com

Fidelity Investments

✉   P.O. Box 770001
   Cincinnati, OH 45277-0001
☎   +1 800 343 3548
💻   www.fidelity.com

Interactive Brokers LLC

✉   Attn: Document Processing
   209 South LaSalle Street
   10th Floor
   Chicago, IL 60604

Interactive Brokers (U.K.) Limited

European customers:

✉   Attn: Document Processing
   P.O. Box 254
   6301 Zug
   Switzerland
☎   +1 877 442 2757
   From Europe: 00800 42 276537
💻   www.interactivebrokers.com

MB Trading, Inc.

✉ 1926 East Maple Avenue
El Segundo, CA 90245
☎ +1 866 628 3001
+1 310 647 4281
🖳 www.mbtrading.com

Robbins Trading Co.

✉ Presidents Plaza
8700 West Bryn Mawr
Seventh Floor, South Tower
Chicago, IL 60631-3507
☎ +1 800 453 4444
+1 773 714 9000
🖳 www.robbinstrading.com

Terra Nova Trading

✉ 100 South Wacker Drive
Suite 1550
Chicago, IL 60606
☎ +1 866 996 8566
🖳 www.terranovatrading.com

Tradestation Securities, Inc.

✉ TradeStation Building
8050 SW 10th Street
Suite 2000
Plantation, FL 33324
☎ +1 800 556 2022
+1 954 652 7000
🖳 www.tradestation.com

Alaron Futures & Options

✉ 822 West Washington Blvd
Chicago, IL 60607
☎ +1 800 275 8844
+1 312 563 8000
💻 www.alaron.com

Global Futures Exchange & Trading Co. Inc.

✉ 16830 Ventura Boulevard
Suite R
Encino, CA 91436
☎ +1 877 367 3177
+1 818 728 0415
💻 www.tradingindex.com

Lind-Waldock

✉ 141 West Jackson Boulevard
Suite 1400-A
Chicago, IL 60604
☎ +1 800 445 2000
+1 312 788 2800
💻 www.lind-waldock.com

TD AMERITRADE Inc.

✉ PO Box 2209
Omaha, NE 68103-2209
New Accounts
PO Box 2760
Omaha, NE 68103-2760
or: 1005 North Ameritrade Place
Bellevue, NE 68005
☎ +1 800 454 9272
Outside U.S.: +1 800 368 3668
From UK: 0500 893 649
💻 www.tdameritrade.com

E*TRADE Group, Inc.

✉ P.O. Box 1542
Merrifield, VA 22116-1542
☎ +1 800 786 2575
Outside U.S.: +44 207 516 1352
🖳 www.etrade.com

OptionsXpress

✉ 39 South LaSalle Street
Suite 220
Chicago, IL 60603
☎ +1 312 630 3300
+1 888 280 8020
🖳 www.optionsxpress.com

Scottrade

✉ PO Box 31759
St. Louis, MO 63131-0759
☎ +1 800 619 SAVE (7283)
🖳 www.scottrade.com

A.G. Edwards & Sons, Inc.

✉ Attn: Contact Center
1 North Jefferson
St. Louis, MO 63103
☎ +1 877 835 7877
🖳 www.agedwards.com

Man Financial Inc.

✉ 141 West Jackson Blvd
Suite 1800A
Chicago, IL 60604
☎ +1 800 621 0265
+1 312 528 3000
🖳 www.manfutures.com

RJOFutures

✉ 222 South Riverside Plaza
Chicago, IL 60606

☎ +1 800 441 1616
+1 800 257 6842
+1 312 373 5478

💻 www.rjofutures.com

Forex.com

✉ 550 Hills Drive
Bedminster, NJ 07921-1539

☎ +1 877 FOREXGO (367 3946)
International: +1 908 731 0750

💻 www.forex.com

FXCM

✉ Forex Capital Markets
Financial Square
32 Old Slip, 10th Floor
New York, NY 10005

☎ +1 888 50 FOREX (36739)
+1 212 201 7301

💻 www.fxcm.com

ChoiceTrade

✉ 197 State Route 18
Suite 3000
East Brunswick, NJ 08816

☎ +1 877 731-9114
+1 732 214-2660

💻 www.choicetrade.com

Just2Trade

✉ 1900 L Street NW Suite 525
Washington, DC 20036
☎ +1 202 386-7261
🖳 www.just2trade.com

Mastertrader.com

✉ 7-11 South Broadway, Suite 210A
White Plains
NY 10601
☎ +1 914 422 2966
🖳 www.mastertrader.com

Zecco

✉ Zecco Trading
P.O. Box 4328
Ontario, CA 91761
☎ +1 877 700 7862
🖳 www.zecco.com

Software platforms

Here I have included institutional and professional platforms that provide services from real-time access to markets, news, fundamental data, analytical tools, charting and analysis.

eSignal

✉ 3955 Point Eden Way
Hayward, CA 94545
☎ +1 510 266 6000
+1 800 815 8256
+1 510 723 1765
In Europe: +44 (0)20 7825 8770
🖥 www.esignal.com
www.futuresource.com

Bloomberg

☎ +1 212 318 2000
Europe: +44 (0)20 7330 7500
🖥 www.bloomberg.com

Reuters

✉ 3 Times Square
New York, NY 10036
☎ +1 646 223 4000
1 800 REUTERS (1 800 738 8377)
🖥 www.reuters.com

Tradestation Securities, Inc.

✉ TradeStation Building
8050 SW 10th Street
Suite 2000
Plantation, FL 33324
☎ (800) 556 2022
(954) 652 7000
🖥 www.tradestation.com

Realtick

✉ Townsend Analytics, Ltd
100 South Wacker Drive
20th Floor
Chicago, IL 60606
☎ +1 800 827 0141
+1 312 621 0141
💻 www.realtick.com

Commodity Systems, Inc. (CSI)

✉ 200 West Palmetto Park Road
Suite 200
Boca Raton, FL 33432
☎ +1 800 274 4727
+1 561 392 8663
💻 www.csidata.com

Software developers

The following includes packages and applications that provide capabilities such as charting tools and indicators, technical or fundamental analysis, systems development capabilities, portfolio management, options analysis, expert systems, and money management. On the market there are a number of companies that develop third-party software plug-ins to implement specific and customized functions. Sometimes, these plug-ins are very powerful and add great value to the software platform.

Advanced Get

✉ eSignal
eSignal Client Services
P.O. Box 5028
Hayward, CA 94540-5028
Europe:
Fitzroy House
13-17 Epworth Street
London, EC2A 4DL
UK
☎ +1 866 367 9296
Outside US: +1 510 723 1737
Europe: +44 (0)20 7825 8770
🖳 www.esignal.com/advancedget

AIQ Trading Expert Pro and AIQ OptionExpert

✉ AIQ Systems
Via UPS or FedEx:
916 Southwood Boulevard Building 3
Incline Village, NV 89452
Via U.S. Post Office:
PO Drawer 7530
Incline Village, NV 89451
☎ +1 800 332 2999
Europe: +44 (0)1707 663700
🖳 www.aiqsystems.com

Amibroker 4.90

Amibroker
💻 www.amibroker.com

Dynamic Trader Software & Trading Course

✉️ 1625 Mid Valley Drive
Suite 86
Steamboat Springs, Colorado 80487
☎ Toll-free: +1 877 382 1618
Outside U.S.: +1 970 879 7351
💻 www.dynamictraders.com

Fibonacci Trader 4 Real Time

✉️ Fibonacci Trader Corporation
450-106 State Road 13 North, #206
Jacksonville, FL 32259-3863
☎ +1 904 260 1515
💻 www.fibonaccitrader.com

Mesa2002

✉️ MESA Software
John Ehlers
6595 Buckley Drive
Cambria, CA 93428
☎ +1 805 927 3065
💻 www.mesasoftware.com

Metastock

✉️ Equis International
90 South 400 West
Suite 620
Salt Lake City, UT 84101
☎ +1 800 508 9180
International: +1 801 265 8886
💻 www.metastock.com

Money Manager 7 and Portfolio Evaluator 7

✉ RINA Systems, Inc.
8180 Corporate Park Drive
Suite 140
Cincinnati, Ohio 45242
☎ +1 513 469 RINA (7462)
💻 www.rinafinancial.com

Neo Ticker 4

✉ TickQuest, Inc.
Corporate Offices
411 Richmond Street East
Suite 2
Toronto, ON
Canada M5A 3S5
☎ +1 416 777 9119
💻 www.tickquest.com

NeuroShell Trader Professional

✉ Ward Systems Group, Inc.
Executive Park West
5 Hillcrest Drive
Frederick, MD 21703
☎ +1 301 662 7950
💻 www.neuroshell.com

Omnitrader

✉ Nirvana Systems, Inc.
7000 North Mopac
Suite 425
Austin, TX 78731
☎ +1 800 880 0338
+1 512 345 2566
💻 www.omnitrader.com

Optionetics.com

✉ Optionetics
255 Shoreline Drive
Suite 100
Redwood City, CA 94065
☎ +1 888 366 8264
+1 650 802 0700
🖥 www.optionetics.com

OptionVue 5

✉ OptionVue Systems International, Inc.
1117 South Milwaukee Avenue
Suite C-10
Libertyville, IL 60048-9860
☎ +1 800 733 6610
+1 847 816 6610
🖥 www.optionvue.com

Telechart 2007

✉ Worden Brothers, Inc.
Five Oaks Office Park
4905 Pine Cone Drive
Durham, NC 27707
☎ +1 800 776 4940
+1 919 408 0542
🖥 www.worden.com

TradingSolutions

✉ NeuroDimension, Inc.
Order Processing Department
3701 NW 40th Terrace
Suite 1
Gainesville, FL 32606
☎ +1 800 634 3327
+1 352 377 5144
🖥 www.tradingsolutions.com

VantagePoint 7.0

✉ Market Technologies, LLC
5807 Old Pasco Road
Wesley Chapel, FL 33544
☎ +1 800 732 5407
International: +1 800 6206 0000
+1 813 973 0496
💻 www.tradertech.com

Tradecision

✉ Alyuda Research
864 Terrace Drive
Los Altos, CA 94024
☎ +1 510 931 7808
+1 888 862 2759 ext. 3
💻 www.tradecision.com

Data providers

Reliable and timely real-time and historical data are fundamental both for trading and back-testing purposes. Professional short-term traders and scalpers need fast real-time data. The average investor may need only historical data to track the stocks of his/her portfolio. The needs are so variegated and different, together with the quality of service provided, that pricing varies from subscriptions of a few dollars up to several hundred dollars per month. You can find real-time/delayed data services. This category includes products that provide a stream of information that is either real time or 15-30 minutes delayed. Most of the trading platform developers also provide data to users. There has been an integration and consolidation process in the past few years that has been putting together the providers of different services such as trading software, brokerage, data, news, and so forth. It is therefore difficult to find companies that only sell data as their core business, but rather you will find data as part of their portfolio of products. You can also find End-Of-Day Data. This category of data services requires the user to initiate the download procedure. With time, more and more data have been made available for free on the internet. For example, you can check with *Yahoo! Finance*, *GoogleFinance* and *MSN Money* as they may provide the information you need.

Bloomberg Professional Service

✉ Bloomberg
🖥 www.bloomberg.com

Interactive Data Real Time

✉ Interactive Data Real-Time Services, Inc.
Global Headquarters
100 Hillside Avenue
White Plains, NY 10603
☎ +1 914 313 4444
+1 800 431 2602
🖥 www.interactivedata-rts.com

QuoteCenter - Reuters DataLink

✉ Equis International
90 South 400 West
Suite 620
Salt Lake City, UT 84101
☎ +1 800 842 3045
+1 800 508 9180
+1 801 265 999
💻 www.equis.com

Prophet Data

✉ Prophet.net
Prophet Financial Systems, Inc.
658 High Street
Palo Alto, CA 94301
☎ +1 800 772 8040
+1 650 322 4183
💻 www.prophet.net

Qcharts

Qcharts
eSignal, Inc.
💻 www.qcharts.com

Reuters Data Feeds

✉ Reuters
3 Times Square
New York, NY 10036
☎ +1 800 REUTERS (1 800 738 8377)
Europe: +1 800 800 700 81
+41 (0)22 722 3633
💻 http://about.reuters.com/productinfo/datafeeds/

IQFeed

✉ DTN Market Access
9110 West Dodge Road
Suite 200
Omaha, NE 68114
☎ +1 800 485 4000
+1 402 390 2328
+1 800 475 4755
💻 www.dtniq.com
www.dtnma.com

CQG

✉ CQG Inc.
Independence Plaza
1050 17th Street
Suite 2000
Denver, CO 80265
☎ +1 800 525 7082
International: +1 44 (0)20 7827 9500
💻 www.cqg.com

Quotrek

✉ eSignal
3955 Point Eden Way
Hayward, CA 94545
☎ +1 510 266 6000
+1 800 815 8256
+1 510 723 1765
Europe: +44 (0)20 7825 8770
💻 www.esignal.com
www.quotrek.com

Pinnacle

✉   Pinnacle Data Corporation
1016 Plank Road
Webster, NY 1458
☎   +1 800 724 4903
+1 585 217 8728
🖳   www.pinnacledata.com

Telechart Gold Service

Worden Brothers Inc.
☎   +1 800 776 4940
🖳   www.worden.com

Unfair Advantage (UA)

✉   Commodity Systems Inc. (CSI)
☎   +1 800 274 4727
🖳   www.csidata.com

Dial-Data

✉   Track Data Corporation
95 Rockwell Place
Brooklyn, NY 11217
☎   +1 718 522 7373
+1 800 275 5544
🖳   www.trackdata.com

Premium Data and Data Tools

Norgate Investor Services
🖳   www.premiumdata.net

Trading Hours

The following information is extracted from the exchanges' websites. I have also provided the link, which is useful as the site provides much more information. Make sure you check the website, to confirm trading hours as they may vary from product to product and change over time. The trading hours I have reported may not be exactly accurate in some cases as I had to summarize them. In reality, futures and options traded both in open auction and electronic markets have different and variable trading hours. Before trading these instruments, you must make sure when markets are open.

New York Stock Exchange

NYSE Arca Equities

Source: www.nyse.com/productservices/nysearcaequities/1157018931781.html

- Pre-opening session: 3:30 - 4.00 ET

- Opening session: 4:00 to 9:30 ET

- Core trading session: 9:30 to 16:00 ET

- Extended hours: 16:00 to 20:00 ET

NYSE Arca Options

Source: www.nyse.com/productservices/nysearcaoptions/1146868213230.html

- Equity Options 9:30 - 16:00 ET

- ETF Options 9:30 - 16:15 ET

Arca Edge – OTC

Source: www.nyse.com/productservices/arcaedge/1157538334897.html

- Pre-open hours: 7:30 - 7:59 ET

- Pre-market hours: 8:00 - 9:29 ET

- Core trading hours: 9:30 - 16:01 ET

NYSE Bonds

Source: www.nyse.com/productservices/securities/1150711905762.html

- Early trading: 4:00 - 9:30 ET

- Core trading: 9:30 - 16:00 ET

- Late trading: 16:00 - 20:00 ET

Bond Auctions

- The NYSE conducts two daily bond auctions:

- Opening Bond Auction at 4:00 ET

- Core Bond Auction at 9:30 ET

The NASDAQ Stock Market

Market Trading Sessions (Eastern Time)

Source: www.nasdaq.com/about/schedule.stm

- Pre-market trading hours: 7:00 - 9:30 ET

- Market hours: 9:30 - 16:00 ET

- After-market hours: 16:00 - 20:00 ET

- Quote and order-entry: 7:00 - 20:00 ET

- Quotes are open and firm: 7:00 - 20:00 ET

American Stock Exchange

The AMEX is open from Monday through Friday 9:30 - 16:00 ET.

Chicago Board of Trade

Source: www.cbot.com/cbot/pub/page/0,3181,932,00.html

On this page, you can find the trading hours and symbols for:

- agricultural
- interest rate
- Dow
- metals products

There are different trading hours for products traded at open auction or electronically, as well as for futures and options.

Agricultural

Futures

- Open Auction: 09:30 - 13:15/13:45 CT

Electronic

Varies according to the product. For many products it is:

- 18:30 - 6:00 CT
- 9:30 - 13:15 CT

Options

- Open Auction: 9:30 - 13:15 CT

Electronic

- 18:35 - 6:00am CT

Interest rate

Futures and options

- Open auction: 7:20 - 14:00 CT
- Electronic: 17:30/18:00 - 16:00 CT

Dow

Futures and options

- Open auction 7:20 - 15:15 (Central Time)

- Electronic varies according to the product

Metals

Options

- Open auction 7:10 - 13:30 CT
- Electronic 18:18 - 416:00 CT

Futures

- Electronic 18:16 - 416:00 CT

The best thing to do is check the website to make sure of the trading hours. They may vary from product to product and change over time.

Chicago Mercantile Exchange

Source: www.cme.com/trading/res/cch/tradehours3497.html

Electronic Globex

Trading is closed from 16:30 to 17:00 CT for CME Equity products, from 15:15 to 17:00 CT for CME Weather products and from 16:00 to 17:00 CT for all other CME products, Monday through Thursday for regularly scheduled maintenance.

Interest rate

*   Sunday 17:00/weekdays 15:30 - Friday 16:00 CT

Equity

*   Sunday 17:00/weekdays 15:30 - Friday 15:15 CT

FX

*   Sunday 15:00/weekdays 15:30 - Friday 16:00 CT

Commodity

*   Check the site because products have different trading hours.

Weather

*   Sunday 17:00/weekdays 17:00 - Friday 15:15 CT

Real estate

*   Sunday 17:00/weekdays 17:00 - Friday 14:00 CT

TRKRS

*   08:30 –15:30 CT

Floor based

Interest rate
- 07:20 - 14:00 CT

Equity
- 08:30 -15:15 CT

FX
- 07:20 - 14:00 CT

Commodity
- 09:05 - 14:00 CT

Weather
- 08:30 - 15:15 CT

Real estate
- 08:00 - 14:00 CT

Be certain to check the site because some products have different trading hours. What I have reported is for general purposes.

Kansas City Board of Trade

Source: www.kcbt.com/symbols_trading_hours.html

Hard red winter wheat futures

- Open Outcry 9:30 - 13:15 CT Monday through Friday

- Electronic 18:32 - 6:00 CT Sunday through Friday and 9:30 - 13:15 CT Monday through Friday

Value Line® stock index futures

- Open Outcry n/a

- Electronic 18:15 - 15:15 CT Sunday through Friday

Hard red winter wheat options

- Open Outcry 9:30 – 13:25 (Central Time) Monday through Friday

- Electronic 18:34 – 6:00 (Central Time) Sunday through Friday

Value Line® stock index options

- Open outcry n/a

- Electronic 18:15 – 15:15 CT Sunday through Friday

New York Mercantile Exchange

Source: www.nymex.com/tradin_hours.aspx

NYMEX Division Physically-Settled Contracts

Open outcry

- 09:00 -1430. Some contracts close between 13:00 and 13:10 CT

CME Globex

- Sunday 18:00 - Friday 17:15 CT

Financially-Settled Contracts on CME Globex®

- Sunday 18:00 - Friday 17:15 CT

COMEX Division

Open Outcry

- Financial CONTRACT
- Trading hours vary from 07:50/08:20 - 13:00/13:30 CT

CME Globex

- Sunday 18:00 - Friday 17:15 CT

Chicago Board of Options Exchange

Source: www.cboe.com/LearnCenter/FaqBasic.aspx

Equities

- 08:30 - 15:00 CT

Indexes

- Trading hours vary depending on the product

You can check the specifications of the product you are interested in at www.cboe.com/Products/default.aspx.

OneChicago

Source: http://onechicago.com/040000_trading/oc_040500.html

Normal trading hours for OneChicago single stock futures and narrow based Indexes are Monday through Friday 8:30– 15:00 CT (15:15 closing for futures on ETFs).

Minneapolis Grain Exchange

Source: www.mgex.com/contract_specs.html

Hard Red Spring Wheat Futures

Open Outcry

- 09:30 - 13:15 Monday through Friday CT

Electronic

- 18:32 - 06:00 Sunday through Friday CT
- 9:30 - 13:15 Monday through Friday CT

Hard red spring wheat options

Open outcry

- 09:30 - 13:30 Monday through Friday CT

Electronic

- 18:34 - 06:00 Sunday through Friday CT

International Securities Exchange

Source: http://phx.corporate-ir.net/phoenix.zhtml?c=176358&p=irol-newsArticle&ID=814957&highlight=

www.ise.com/WebForm/viewPage.aspx?categoryId=194&header1=true&menu3=true

- 9:30 - 16:00 Monday through Friday ET

Trading is extended to 16:15 for ETFs that trade for the 15m extended period.

IntercontinentalExchange

Source: www.theice.com/publicdocs/support/support_cal.pdf

ICE Futures U.S. markets – Electronic and Floor

Check the website. Trading hours vary a lot depending on the product and whether it is traded electronically or on the floor.

The Chicago Stock Exchange

Source: www.chx.com/content/Trading_Information/matchingsys.html

Regular trading session

- 08:30 – 15:00 CT. Some exchange-traded funds shall trade until 15:15.

Late trading session

- It will start immediately after the close until 15:30.

Boston Stock Exchange

Source: www.bostonstock.com/BostonstockPDF/Legal/filings/BSE_Rules_6.7.07.pdf at page 66

www.bostonstock.com/BostonstockPDF/Legal/filings/BOX_RULES_6_28_07.pdf at page 49

Primary session

- 09:30 - 16:00 ET

Post primary session

- 16:00 - 16:15 ET

After-hours

- 16:15 - 17:00 ET

Philadelphia Stock Exchange

Source: www.phlx.com/exchange/trhours.html

Equities

Core session

- 9:30 - 16:00 ET. 16:15 p.m. for some ETFs

Pre-market session

- 8:00 - 09:30 ET

Post market session

- 16:00 - 18:00 ET

Equity options

- 9:30 - 16:00 ET.

16:15 p.m. for some ETFs index options

- Narrow-based – 9:30 - 16:00 ET
- Broad-based – 9:30 - 16:15 ET

U.S. dollar settled world currency options

- 9:30 - 16:00 ET

National Stock Exchange

Source: www.nsx.com/pricing_faq.html

Open from 8:00 –18:30 (Eastern Time)

Glossary

Active management: The process of using techniques to pursue investment returns in order to outperform a benchmark index.

Alpha: Measure of risk-adjusted performance. When related to a mutual fund, it measures the excess returns compared with excess returns of a benchmark.

Annual and semi-annual reports: Records sent to shareholders that discuss a fund's performance and identify the securities in the fund's portfolio on a specific date. When referring to a company, it is a record of a company's financial condition. It describes the firm's operations, balance sheet, income statement, and cash-flow statement information.

Arbitrage: The simultaneous buying and selling of an asset in two different markets to pursue a profit without risk. Arbitrage opportunities are often precluded by transactions costs.

Arbitration: An alternative to the court system in settling disputes over transactions.

Ask: It is the lowest price an investor will accept to sell an asset.

Asset allocation: The process of apportioning investments among various asset classes, such as stocks, bonds, commodities, etc.

Assets: Any possession that has value in an exchange.

At-the-money: An option is said to be "at-the-money" if the strike price of the option is equal to the market price of the underlying security.

Auction market: Markets in which price is determined through the interaction of buyers and sellers, such as floor brokers and specialists on the floor of a stock exchange.

Auditor: An examination of a company's accounting records and books conducted by a certified public accountant.

Back office: Brokerage's clerical operations that support the trading of stocks and other securities.

Backwardation: In this situation futures prices are lower in the distant delivery months than in the nearest delivery month. It is the opposite of contango.

Balance sheet: A summary of the value of a company's assets, liabilities, and ownership equity on a specific date.

Bankruptcy risk: The risk associated to a firm's inability to meet its debt obligations (default).

Basis: The difference between the spot/cash price and the futures price of the nearest expiring contract of the underlying instrument.

Bear: It is related to an investor, a strategy or a trend that refers to a declining market.

Benchmark: A standard index or predetermined set of assets used for measuring the performance of an investment.

Beta: A coefficient used to measure the volatility of a fund, a stock or a portfolio relative to a market index or other benchmark.

Bid: The highest price an investor will accept to buy an asset.

Blue chip: A large and creditworthy company known for the quality of its management, products or services and that has stable earnings and pays regular dividends.

Bond: A debt security issued by a company, municipality, or government agency. An investor lends money to the issuer and, in exchange, the issuer pays an interest and promises to repay the loan amount on a specified maturity date.

Broker: An agent that executes orders on behalf of financial and commercial institutions and/or the public and who is paid a commission or a fee for executing the transactions.

Bull: It is related to an investor, a strategy, a trend or any other concept that refers to a rising market.

Buying power: The amount of money available to buy securities. It is determined by adding the cash held in the account and the amount that could be spent on margin.

Call option: An option that gives the buyer the right, but not the obligation, to purchase the underlying stock or futures contract at the strike price on or before the expiration date.

Cash market: Also called a spot market, where investors buy and sell securities or instruments that involve the immediate delivery.

Cash settlement: A transaction in which a contract is settled in cash on the same trade day.

Certificate of deposit (CD): An agreement with a bank or thrift that you will leave your money on deposit for a specified period of time in return for a specific amount of interest.

Clear: The process by which a clearing house matches the buyer and seller record and confirms that the counterparts agree to the terms.

Clearing house: It is the center of a market through which transactions are cleared. It acts as the counterpart to the buyer and the seller. It ensures that underlying instruments are delivered and maintains the margin accounts.

Closed-end fund: An investment company that has a fixed number of shares that are publicly traded. The price of a closed-end fund share fluctuates based on investor supply and demand throughout the day over an exchange.

Closing Price: Price of the last transaction of an asset executed during a trading session on an exchange.

Closing range: The high and low prices recorded during the period designated as the official close (see also settlement).

Commission: The fee an investor pays to a broker to buy or sell a security for his account.

Commodity: A natural raw material or other product that can be used for commerce. Commodities are traded on a commodity exchange. They include agricultural products, metals, petroleum, and so forth.

Common stock: They represent ownership in a company. Investors have voting rights at stockholders' meetings. They are entitled to receive dividends. If a company fails, they have the last claim on assets and income of a company, after other creditors have been paid.

Contango: In this situation, futures prices are higher the further the maturity date. It is the opposite of backwardation.

Contract month: A specific month in which futures contracts are satisfied. Also known as the delivery month.

Convertible arbitrage: Investment strategy that intends to exploit inefficiencies between a convertible bond and the underlying stock. It consists in buying convertible bonds and selling short the equivalent of the underlying shares.

Creation unit: The minimum block of ETF shares that can be bought or sold from the fund company at net asset value.

Credit risk: The possibility that a bond issuer may not be able to pay interest or repay its debt.

Day traders: Traders who open trading positions and close them prior to the close of the same trading day.

Dealer: An entity (an individual or a company) that trades financial instruments and takes positions for its own account.

Delta: It is a measure of price sensitivity of options. It measures how much a price changes for one unit of change in the underlying instrument.

Derivative: An investment tool whose value depends on the value of the underlying instrument. Futures contracts, options and swaps are types of derivatives.

Distressed securities investing: Strategy focused on troubled or restructuring companies through stocks, bonds, bank debt, etc.

Diversification: Minimizing of non-systematic risk with a portfolio composed of securities whose returns present different risks and correlations.

Dividend: A portion of a company's after-tax profit paid out to shareholders.

Dollar-Cost Averaging: Strategy of investing a fixed amount of money at regular intervals.

Emerging markets investing: A generally long-only strategy of investing in markets of developing economies usually characterized by high growth rates.

Equity market neutral investing: Equity investing on both the long and short side, with equal dollar amounts. It is used to neutralize market risk. Picking the right stocks is all that matters because the investor attempts to identify the strongest and the weakest stocks within the same sector, industry and so forth.

EBITDA: Earnings Before Interest, Taxes, Depreciation, and Amortization.

Efficient market hypothesis: The theory that relevant information is immediately reflected in an asset's market price not allowing for abnormal market returns due to inefficiencies.

Event-driven investing: Strategy seeking to exploit security pricing inefficiencies that may occur because of some sort of corporate event such as a merger, takeover, restructure, and so forth.

Excess margin: Equity in an account above the minimum required for meeting the initial margin or the maintenance requirement.

Exchange-Traded Fund (ETF): The broad class of funds that trade throughout the day over an exchange, legally classified as open-end companies or unit investment trusts, and track an index, a commodity, a sector, etc.

Exercise: Action taken by the holder of a call option to purchase the underlying instrument, or by the holder of a put option to sell the underlying instrument.

Expense ratio: Percentage of a mutual fund or ETF assets spent to do business, including management and advisory fees, and overhead costs. It does not include commissions you pay to buy and sell ETF shares or costs incurred by a fund to trade its securities.

Expiration date: In case of options, it is the last day on which an option can be either exercised or offset. After expiration, the option rights cease to exist.

Face value (par value or maturity value): It is the amount that a bond's issuer agrees to repay at the maturity date.

Fill or kill: It is an order that must be filled immediately or cancelled.

Financial instruments: Instruments classified generally as equity-based or debt-based.

Fixed-income: It is related to debt instruments (e.g. bonds), which make periodic interest payments providing regular returns.

Fixed-income arbitrage: Strategy that seeks to exploit pricing inefficiencies in fixed income securities and their derivative instruments.

Fixed-income directional: Strategy aimed at investing in fixed income instruments investing on the long or short side.

Floor broker: Exchange member who is paid a fee to execute buy or sell orders for clients, acting as agent on the floor of the exchange.

Floor trader: Member of an exchange who executes trades for his own account or for an account controlled by him.

Fund of funds: Investment partnership that invests in a series of other funds.

Futures: Agreement to undertake the purchase and sale of financial instruments or physical commodities for future delivery at a fixed price on an exchange. Futures contracts are standardized, according to the quality, quantity, delivery time and location, which are traded at authorized exchanges.

Futures commission merchant: An individual or legal entity registered with the Commodity Futures Trading Commission that solicits or accepts and handles orders to buy or sell futures contracts or options on futures and accepts money or other assets from customers to margin such orders.

Futures exchange: A marketplace with rules and regulations where buyers and sellers can trade contracts for future delivery of commodities and financial instruments.

Growth stock: Stock of a corporation that displays high price/earnings ratio because of its high expected earnings growth.

Hedge fund: A private investment pool for accredited investors that seeks to make a positive return investing in financial instruments and pursuing leveraging and other speculative investment practices. Unlike a mutual fund, a hedge fund is exempt from registering with the SEC.

Hedge: It is used to reduce the market fluctuation price risk. An example would be to build opposite positions in the cash market and futures market at the same time.

Hurdle-rate: The investment return that a fund must exceed before a performance related fee can be charged.

Initial margin: The amount an investor has to pay to a clearing house in order to place an order to buy or sell a futures contract and to protect the counterpart against the execution of the transaction. Referring to stocks, it is the percentage of the purchase price of securities that can be purchased on margin.

Initial Public Offering (IPO): The first offering of stock to the public by a privately owned corporation.

In-the-money: A call option is said to be "in the money" if the option strike price is below the underlying security's price. For a put option it is the opposite.

Investment company: A firm that invests pooled shareholder money in securities appropriate for their stated investment objectives in return for a management fee. Mutual funds, closed-end funds, and unit investment trusts are types of investment companies.

Issuer: Company, municipality, government agency or other legal entity that issues a security, such as a stock, bond, or other.

Junk bonds: High-risk high-yield bonds, who are rated below investment grade by credit agencies, with a credit rating of BB or lower.

Large-cap stocks: Stocks of large-capitalization companies; they usually have a $10 billion market value.

Leverage: The use of financial instruments, such as an options or futures contract, to increase the potential return of an investment. As a measure of cash spent to purchase, compared with the value of the underlying position, it magnifies both gains and losses.

Limit order: An order in which the customer sets the maximum price for a buy order and the minimum for a sell.

Liquid: A characteristic of a market to allow large transactions without a significant change in price.

Maintenance margin: A minimum margin that a client must maintain in his margin account in order to continue to hold a position. Maintenance margin is typically less than the initial margin, and also differs by futures contract. Referring stocks it is the minimum amount of equity in your margin account required after you buy stock on margin.

Managed futures account: An account managed by a commodity trading advisor, generally investing in futures markets.

Margin: It refers to buying securities by borrowing money from a broker/dealer. It represents the difference between the market value of the security and the loan.

Margin call: A call from a brokerage firm to a customer or a clearing-house to a member, to restore margin deposit in the account to the required level.

Market-neutral investing: Investing in financial markets through a strategy that will result in an investment portfolio not correlated to overall market movements and insulated from systematic market risk.

Medium-cap securities: Equity securities with a middle-level stock market capitalization.

Market order: An order to buy or sell to be filled at the best possible price and as soon as possible.

Mark-to-market: The process of debiting or crediting clients' margin accounts on a daily basis according to the settlement price of the trading session.

Maturity: The date when an issuer has to repay the bond's face value.

Money manager: A portfolio/investment manager.

Mutual fund: An investment company that buys a selected group of assets to meet stated financial objectives.

Narrow-based index futures: An index based on industry sector, focused to a specific sector, such as auto, utilities, or telecom industries.

NAV: Net Asset Value. It is the market value of a fund/ETF share. It equals the closing market value of all securities within a portfolio less any liabilities divided by the number of outstanding shares.

Nearby (delivery) month: The futures contract month closest to expiration.

No-load fund: A mutual fund whose shares are sold without a sales commission.

Offset: To liquidate a futures or option (at any time prior to expiration) position by making a transaction opposite to the initial or opening position.

Open auction: Method of trading where buyers and sellers on a trading floor make verbal bids and offers.

Open interest: The accumulated total number of outstanding futures or options contracts of a given product that have not yet been offset.

Open-End Investment Company: The typical mutual-fund structure, which is ready to redeem its shares from investors on any business day and create new shares on demand.

Opening Range: A range of prices at which transactions take place at the opening of the market.

Option: A contract that conveys the right, but not the obligation, to buy or sell a particular underlying instrument at a certain price at any time prior to a specified date.

Option premium: The sum of money that the option buyer pays and the option seller receives for the rights granted by the option.

Out-of-the-money: A call option is said to be "out-the-money" when the current price of the underlying instrument is above the strike price. For a put it is the opposite.

Physical delivery: The transfer of the underlying commodity from the seller of a futures contract to the buyer of a futures contract.

Portfolio: A collection of securities owned by an individual or an institution.

Preferred stock: A class of stock with a claim on the company's earnings before payment may be made on common stock and is usually entitled to priority over common stockholders if the company fails or liquidates. Preferred stock normally does not have voting rights.

Prospectus: The official document that describes a mutual fund to prospective investors. It contains information required by the SEC.

Put option: An option that gives the option buyer the right but not the obligation to sell short the underlying stock or futures contract at the strike price on or before the expiration date.

Rate of return: Percentage appreciation in value for a security or portfolio.

Redeem: To cash in mutual-fund shares by selling them back to the fund.

Redemption fee: It is a fee charged upon a voluntary redemption from an investment fund.

Scalper: A trader who trades for very small, short-term profits during a trading session.

Settle (settlement price): Typically refer to futures. It is the official daily closing price; normally it is the closing price or the midpoint of the closing range on any trading day.

Single-stock futures: An agreement to commit one party to buy a stock and one party to sell a stock at a given price and on a specified date. They are similar to futures contracts.

Small-cap: Securities in which the parent company's total stock-market capitalization is less than $2 billion.

Soft commodities: Commodities such as coffee, sugar and cocoa. It may also include cotton, oilseeds, grains, and orange juice.

Sovereign debt: Fixed income security guaranteed by a foreign government.

Spiders: Standard & Poor's Depository Receipts (SPDR) are a group of ETFs that track a variety of Standard & Poor's indexes.

Spread: It is the difference in a price quotation between the bid and the ask.

Stock: A share of ownership or equity in a corporation.

Stock market: A market in which shares of stock are bought and sold.

Stop order: An order to buy or sell when the market reaches a specified point.

Stop-limit order: A variation of a stop order in which a trade must be executed at the exact price or better.

Strike price (exercise price): The price at which the underlying instrument of a call or put option can be purchased (if a call) or sold (if a put).

Tick: The smallest allowable increment of price movement for an instrument.

Trading limit (position limit): The maximum number of futures contracts that can be held as determined by the Commodity Futures Trading Commission and/or the exchange.

Unit investment trust (UIT): An investment company that buys and holds a fixed number of shares until the trust's termination date. This is a structure used by some ETFs.

Bibliography

Writing this book I have conducted extensive research on the internet. I intended *Trading the U.S. Markets* as a guide for beginners and more advanced traders. In this regard, I included a high number of internet links to help and encourage readers to look and find more detailed information on the web. Nowadays, the internet provides an immense resource of information available to everyone. Interaction between the book and the websites I mentioned as a reference in every chapter can be useful to improve the readers' knowledge of the financial environment. Markets evolve continuously. Although tracking these changes is quite difficult, it is also exciting as market regulations adapt to new situations, players change their strategies adapting them to the new environment, and the public try to find the best way to approach markets to speculate, build their pension plan, and invest for their future.

Barry Rudd. *Stock Patterns for Day Trading II: Advanced Techniques (Stock Patterns for Day Trading)*. Traders Press (1999)

Brett N. Steenbarger. *Enhancing Trader Performance: Proven Strategies From the Cutting Edge of Trading Psychology*. Wiley (2006)

Frank J.S. Fabozzi. *Bond Markets, Analysis and Strategies*. Prentice Hall (2006)

Jack D. Schwager. *A Complete Guide to the Futures Markets: Fundamental Analysis, Technical Analysis, Trading, Spreads, and Options*. Wiley (1984)

Jason Kelly. *The Neatest Little Guide to Stock Market Investing*. Plume (2007)

Joel Greenblatt. *The Little Book That Beats the Market*. Wiley (2005)

John C. Hull. *Options, Futures and Other Derivatives*. Prentice Hall (2005)

John M. Dalton. *How The Stock Market Works*. Prentice Hall Press (2001)

Larry Harris. *Trading and Exchanges: Market Microstructure for Practitioners*. Oxford University Press, USA (2002)

Laurence A. Connors, Linda Bradford Raschke. *Street Smarts: High Probability Short-Term Trading Strategies*. M. Gordon Publishing Group (1996)

Louis C. Engel, Henry R. Hecht. *How to Buy Stocks*. Little (1994)

Martin J. Pring. *Technical Analysis Explained: The Successful Investor's Guide to Spotting Investment Trends and Turning Points*. McGraw-Hill (2002)

Paul Heyne, Peter J. Boettke, and David L. Prychitko. *The Economic Way of Thinking*. Prentice Hall (2005)

Philip J. McDonnell. *Optimal Portfolio Trading*. Wiley (2008)

Richard J. Teweles, Frank J. Jones. *The Futures Game: Who Wins, Who Loses, & Why*. McGraw-Hill (1998)

Robert A. Schwartz, Reto Francioni. *Equity Markets in Action: The Fundamentals of Liquidity, Market Structure & Trading*. Wiley (2004)

Van K. Tharp. *Trade Your Way to Financial Freedom*. McGraw-Hill (2006)

Victor Niederhoffer, Laurel Kenner. *Practical speculation*. Wiley (2005)

Victor Niederhoffer, Laurel Kenner. *The Education of a Speculator*. Wiley (1998)

Index

A

account (broking) 111
AEMI (Auction & Electronic Market Integration) 12
after hours trading 15, 17, 85, 88
algorithmic trading 4, 37, 124, 187-188
American Depositary Receipt (ADR) 59, 61
American Stock Exchange (AMEX) 5, 11, 21, 193, 218
ANTE (AMEX New Trading Environment) 12
arbitrage 49, 50, 188
ask 86, 92, 117, 176-177
Automated Bond System® (ABS) 8
automated trading 39, 187

B

BARS (Booth Automated Routing System) 12
BBSS (Broker Booth Support System) 6
bankruptcy 135,
Best Bid Offer (BBO) 176
best execution 81-83
bid 10, 12, 82, 86, 100, 173, 176
bid/ask spread 68, 91, 93, 117, 169, 176-177
blogs 149-152
Blue Sky Laws 145
bonds 40, 44-45, 57, 76-78

bond funds 45
Boston Stock Exchange (BSE) 10, 27, 29, 207, 227
broker-directed trading 105
broker default 132
brokers 5, 10, 99, 197
brokered markets 40-41
bulletin board 26, 33
Buttonwood Agreement 4

C

cash account 114, 124
Central Registration Depository (CRD) 104
charts 100, 159-160
Chicago Board of Trade (CBOT) 3, 13-15, 17-18, 193
Chicago Board Options Exchange (CBOE) 3, 13, 20-23, 90, 95, 194
Chicago Mercantile Exchange (CME) 3, 14-15, 193
Chicago Stock Exchange (CHX) 27-28, 195, 227
clearing 15-16, 19, 63-64, 88-91
closed-end fund 11, 43, 46
Closing Cross electronic auction 10
commission 4, 56, 68, 86, 99, 100-102, 109, 117
Commitments of Traders (COT) report 67
Commodity Exchange (COMEX) 18-19, 224
Commodity Futures Modernization Act of 2000 (CFMA) 23, 64, 73

International Securities Exchange
(ISE) 21, 24, 27, 195
intraday 159-160, 162, 168, 181
investment adviser 47-48, 103,
136, 141, 144
Investment Adviser Registration
Depository (IARD) 141
Investor Protection Trust (IPT) 140

J

junk bonds 77
Joint Asian Derivatives Exchange
(JADE) 14

K

Kansas City Board of Trade
(KCBT) 3, 14, 17-18, 194

L

large caps 44, 50, 54, 57
limit order 29, 37, 41, 82-83, 85,
92, 105, 109, 169, 172-174, 177-
179
liquidity 12, 40, 49, 53, 63, 81, 83-
84, 86, 91-93, 172, 176-177
Long-term Equity AnticiPation Securities (LEAPS) 20, 31, 71-72

M

Magazines 108, 149, 155-156
maintenance margin 123, 126-127
margin 65-66, 68, 91, 113, 119,
124
    account 91, 113-114, 119,
    125-126
    call 65, 68, 91, 125-126
market
    hours 83, 86
    if-touched 174
    integrity 81-83

    maker 6, 23, 34, 105-106
    neutral 49-50, 72
    order 82, 92, 101, 105, 172,
    174, 178
mean absolute 93
Minneapolis Grain Exchange
(MGEX) 3, 24, 194
money-market fund 46, 119
mutual fund 43-44, 46-47, 53, 56-
57, 121

N

National Association of Securities
Dealers Quotations (NASDAQ) 8
    NASDAQ Global Market
    Companies 9
    NASDAQ Capital Market
    Companies 9
    NASDAQ Global Select
    Market Companies 9
    NASDAQ Integrated System
    10
    NASDAQ Market Center 8-
    10, 38
National Stock Exchange (NSX)
32
NASDAQ, see 'National Associa-
tion of Securities Dealers Auto-
mated
Quotations'
National Futures Association
(NFA) 138
National Market System 3, 28, 37,
53, 147
National Securities Clearing Cor-
poration (NSCC) 89
net asset value (NAV) 46, 56-57
NETS (New Equity Trading Sys-
tem) 12
New York Board of Trade Ex-
change (NYBOT) 3, 14, 20, 26